*The Strains of
Economic Growth:
Labor Unrest and Social
Dissatisfaction in Korea*

Harvard Studies in International Development

*Jointly published by the International Center for Economic Growth.

The Strains of Economic Growth: Labor Unrest and Social Dissatisfaction in Korea

David L. Lindauer
Jong-Gie Kim
Joung-Woo Lee
Hy-Sop Lim
Jae-Young Son
Ezra F. Vogel

Harvard Institute for International Development
and Korea Development Institute

Distributed by Harvard University Press

Published by the Harvard Institute for International Development
March, 1997

Distributed by Harvard University Press

Editorial management: Don Lippincott
Editorial assistance: Jolanta Davis
Design and production: Editorial Services of New England, Inc.

Library of Congress Cataloging-in-Publication Data

The strains of economic growth: labor unrest and social
    dissatisfaction in Korea/David L. Lindauer . . . [et al.].
        p. cm. — (Harvard studies in international development)
    Includes bibliographical references and index.
    ISBN 0-674-83981-1 (cloth)
    1. Korea (South)—Economic conditions—1960– 2. Korea (South)—
Social conditions. 3. Labor disputes—Korea (South) 4. Social
conflict—Korea (South) I. Lindauer, David L., 1952–   .
II. Harvard Institute for International Development.   III. Han 'guk
Kaebal Yŏn 'guwŏn.   IV. Title: Labor unrest and social
dissatisfaction in Korea V. Series.
HC467.S77   1997
338.95193—dc21   97-5513
                                                                     CIP

Printed in the United States of America

Dedicated to Michael Roemer
(1937 – 1996)

Contents

Contributors

David L. Lindauer is Professor of Economics at Wellesley College in Massachusetts, and a Faculty Associate of the Harvard Institute for International Development. His research focuses on labor markets in developing economies. Professor Lindauer often consults for the World Bank and was a member of the Core Team responsible for the 1995 *World Development Report, Workers in an Integrating World*. He is co-editor of *Asia and Africa: Legacies and Opportunities in Development* (1994) and *Rehabilitating Government: Pay and Employment Reform in Africa* (1994). Professor Lindauer received his Ph.D. in economics from Harvard University.

Jong-Gie Kim is the President of the Korea Environmental Technology Research Institute in Seoul. Previously, he was Senior Fellow and Director of Research Coordination at the Korea Development Institute. Dr. Kim has conducted extensive research on regional development policy. He is the editor of *Regional Industrial Development Policy* (1987) and *Regional Development Strategy: A Study of Cheju Island* (1989). Dr. Kim received an M.A. in Urban Planning from the University of Washington and a Ph.D. in regional economics from Cornell University.

Joung-Woo Lee is Professor of Economics and Chairman of the Department of Economics at the School of Economics and Trade, Kyungpook National University, Daegu, Korea. He has written widely in the areas of income distribution, poverty, and labor. He is the coauthor of *Policies toward the Urban Poor* (1989) and author of *Income Distribution Economics* (1991). In 1992–1993 Professor Lee was a Visiting Scholar at the Harvard-Yenching Institute. He received his Ph.D. in economics from Harvard University.

Hy-Sop Lim is Professor of Sociology at Korea University. He is also President of the Korean Social Science Research Council and has served as President of the Korean Sociological Association. He has written extensively on the subject of social change and development. He is the author of *Social Change and Cultural Change* (1984), *Development and Social Equality* (1985), and *Social Change and Values in Korea* (1994). Professor Lim holds a Ph.D. in sociology from Emory University.

Jae-Young Son is Associate Professor and Chairman, Department of Real Estate, Kon-Kuk University, Seoul, Korea. Previously, he served as a Fellow at the Korea Development Institute and as a Fellow at the Korea Research Institute for Human Settlement. Professor Son is the editor of *Analyses of Land Market and Land Policy Alternatives* (1993). He received his Ph.D. in economics from the University of California at Berkeley.

Ezra F. Vogel is Henry Ford II Professor of the Social Sciences and Director of the John K. Fairbank Center for East Asian Research at Harvard University. From 1993 to 1995 he served as National Intelligence Officer for East Asia at the National Intelligence Council. Among his many books and articles are *Japan's New Middle Class* (1963), *One Step Ahead in China: Guangdong Under Reform* (1989), and *The Four Little Dragons: The Spread of Industrialization in East Asia* (1991). Professor Vogel has received numerous honorary degrees and received his Ph.D. from Harvard University.

Preface

Nearly twenty years ago the Korea Development Institute (KDI) and the Harvard Institute for International Development (HIID) began a joint research project that resulted in the publication of ten book-length studies on the first three decades of Korean economic development (1945–1975). The positive reception afforded these volumes, combined with significant new developments in the Korean economy, encouraged the two institutes to think of a sequel. We decided to focus on a number of studies that went in-depth into several features of the post-1975 period.

Three themes were chosen that dealt with central features of Korean development, which either were not present in the pre-1975 period or were present only in muted form. The first of these studies dealt with macroeconomic policy during the 1970s, when oil prices rose sharply, and with the aftermath of these macro adjustments in the 1980s. The second study dealt with Korea's movement away from generalized support for exports of manufactures to a policy of targeting specific industries, the heavy and chemical industry drive of 1973–1979, to a retreat from industrial targeting in the 1980s. This, the third and final study, deals with some of the strains of rapid economic growth. Special attention is paid to the labor market and labor relations in the 1980s, when Korea's democratization led to the end of government efforts to suppress the labor movement, and workers and management had to learn new ways of working together.

These three studies differ from the earlier ten-volume series in another important respect. The earlier series dealt only peripherally with the politics of the economic changes that were analyzed. The three recent studies include political economy issues as central themes. Technical economic analysis continues to play an important role, but many chapters are devoted to how and why key economic policy decisions were actually made, a process that involved more than purely economic considerations.

This volume begins by recognizing that despite all its spectacular economic achievements, Korean society was in a state of crisis in the late 1980s. Nowhere was this more evident than in the unrest surrounding labor relations. In the two months of July and August 1987, Korean workers initiated more strikes than had been recorded in the previous quarter of a century. As the nation prepared for the summer Olympics of 1988, scenes of riot police battling Korean workers could be seen on the nightly news around the world.

Despite low unemployment and rapidly increasing real wages, Korea's workers—the backbone of the nation's export-led growth—challenged the nation's prevailing system of labor relations and demanded *a voice* that long had been denied them. Many factors contributed to their dissatisfaction and that of many Korean households. There was widespread desire for greater political freedoms and, in a society with an historical intolerance for inequality, growing concentration in the distribution of wealth met with broad social disapproval and deep resentment. Workers had additional grievances. Real wages and employment had grown rapidly, but the conditions of working life were slow to improve. Hours remained extraordinarily long, industrial safety poor, and independent representation virtually nonexistent.

One of the conclusions of this study is that Korea did well in relying on competitive forces to determine wages and employment outcomes. But the historical suppression of labor organizations limited improvements in the quality of working life and contributed to the labor unrest that marred the performance of the economy and strained the nation's social fabric.

In completing this volume, the last in the sequel, we wish to thank David Lindauer who bore principal responsibility for managing the research for all three volumes. We also want to thank the four past presidents of KDI who helped initiate these studies and bring them to fruition, Dr. Park Yung Chul, Dr. Koo Bon Ho, Dr. Song Hee Yhon, and Dr. Whang In-Joung. Special thanks are owed Dwight H. Perkins, former Director of HIID, who also helped initiate these studies and who actively participated in all phases of the research. Funding for these studies was provided from KDI funds and from the unrestricted income of HIID.

This volume benefited from the able research assistance of Kim Hong-Jin. We also acknowledge the contributions of Allison Brucker, Deborah McCarthy, Amy Sanders, and Patricia Sjostedt in helping to prepare the manuscript. The editorial management of this volume was under the overall direction of Don Lippincott of HIID's publications office, with the assistance of Jolanta Davis. Special thanks are also due Lauren Byrne and her associates at Editorial Services of New England for their fine work on all three volumes.

Jeffrey D. Sachs
Director, HIID

Dong-Se Cha
President, KDI

1

Introduction

David L. Lindauer

By the end of the 1980s, the strains accompanying Korea's rapid economic growth were visible throughout the society. Growth had resulted in an increasingly complex economy that many thought was beyond the capabilities of government to manage. Despite the success achieved under decades of heavy government intervention, there were widespread calls for less government involvement and more economic liberalization, especially in the financial sector. Along with success in export markets came external pressures to open the economy. But domestic interest groups, from farmers to automobile producers, resisted such changes, preferring to maintain the advantages under which they had prospered. The *chaebol*, long seen as a pillar of the Korean economic miracle, came under attack for their excessive wealth and influence.

Korean households, most of which had realized unprecedented gains in family income, expressed anger over what they perceived as growing income inequality and the illegitimate gains of the nation's business elite. Environmental degradation, a by-product of relatively unregulated industrial growth, became a significant issue, as did the call for social welfare legislation to protect the poor and vulnerable. And finally, past economic gains were no longer enough; in the 1980s Koreans demanded an increase in political freedom to accompany their new material prosperity.

The strains that accompanied rapid economic growth are not unique to Korea. Other fast-growing economies have experienced similar tensions. Japan went through a comparable phase in the 1960s.[1] In Taiwan, environmental issues and pro-democracy movements were prominent in the 1980s. And there are parallels between Korea's experience in the 1980s and social discontent in Indonesia in the mid-1990s. In all cases, rapid growth brought about social dislocation and a realignment of social classes, breeding grounds for dissatisfaction and discontent. Income inequality and market failure also seemed to confront growing intolerance.[2]

This book seeks to provide a better understanding of the roots of discontent among Korea's workers and other social groups. We pay particular attention to workers because the strains accompanying Korean economic growth are nowhere more evident than in labor relations. Labor unrest and worker dissatisfaction existed in earlier decades, but starting in mid-1987 the degree of militant behavior and the depth of worker anger seemed historically unprecedented. What is surprising about these developments is that no other nation has ever recorded as rapid and as sustained an increase in average wages and industrial employment opportunities as has the post-1965 Korean economy. Korean workers shared in the nation's growing prosperity, but dissatisfaction dominated their attitudes and fueled their militant actions.

By better understanding the roots of social dissatisfaction in Korea, we hope to assist Korean policymakers in working toward longer-term resolutions of social conflict, especially among workers, managers, and government. Beyond the nation's borders, a better understanding of what happened in Korea may help identify the sources of social tension other countries may anticipate when seeking to emulate Korea's development strategy.

Politics and Distribution

No single factor can account for worker dissatisfaction in the 1980s or for the economic discontent expressed by other social groups. Political, social, and economic determinants all played a role. In this opening chapter, attention is given to two basic arguments that might explain the responses of Korean workers: the lack of political freedoms and the uneven distribution of the benefits of economic growth.

Korean workers—in fact the majority of Koreans—had limited political freedom for most of this century. Even with sustained economic progress, civil liberties—the demand for which tends to rise with income—had not been forthcoming during the Park (1963–1979) and Chun (1981–1987) presidencies. The failure of Korea's modernization to deliver more democratic institutions has been traced to many factors, including the legacy of a traditional society based on centralized rule under an autocratic monarch; the uncontrolled way social change took place under colonization, totally dismantling existing political institutions and forcing Koreans to start from the very beginning in the aftermath of liberation; the failure of early experiments in modern politics, including the leadership of Syngman Rhee and the parliamentary democracy of

1960–1961; and the threat from the North, which demanded a strong state capable of meeting any challenge.[3]

Given the long absence of political rights and the historical exclusion of labor from Korean politics, it is no coincidence that labor unrest followed directly on the heels of the political liberalization initiated by President Roh Tae-Woo's proclamation of June 1987.[4] However, the dissatisfaction among Korean workers—perhaps unlike that among students, teachers, journalists, and other intellectuals—was driven by more than a desire for political freedoms and participation. Politics mattered, although a workers' party was not a common demand among industrial labor; labor more often railed against the economic and social consequences of the nation's growth-first strategy. Feeling left out, workers demanded union representation, higher wages, and better treatment by their employers.

The feeling of being left out, or left behind, raises the question of distribution—of how growth was shared. Different dimensions of distribution occupy subsequent chapters; here economy-wide patterns are assessed. In the mid-1960s, at the start of rapid growth, Korea's distribution of income was relatively equal by international standards—the result of nearly five decades of exploitative colonial rule, widespread poverty in the aftermath of civil war and reconstruction, and the progressive land reform undertaken in the late 1940s. Between 1970 and 1980, the distribution of income worsened (Table 1-1). The Heavy and Chemical Industry drive of this period played a role, fostering a high-income group of urban professionals and owners of capital. According to Economic Planning Board (EPB) estimates, the distribution of income in the 1980s reversed course and again became more equal, a trend that would continue into the 1990s. By 1988, when labor unrest was overwhelming the country, Korea's Gini coefficient was estimated at .336, virtually identical to its 1970 value, .332, when the economy is considered to have realized one of its most equal outcomes. These numbers do not support labor's view of having been left out or left behind, even in a relative sense.

Is something missing in the data? Household surveys used to estimate income distribution in Korea are known to have systematically excluded the incomes of both the poor and the rich. In some years, as many as 40 percent of all households, including the extremes of the distribution, were missing or inadequately represented. Independent surveys and estimates, including a 1988 Korea Development Institute survey, suggest more income inequality than is reported by the EPB estimate (Table 1-1). Official estimates may suggest more equality than actually existed, but

Table 1-1. The Distribution of Income in Korea, 1965–1993

Percentage of Households	Percentage of Income						
	1965	1970	1976	1980	1985	1988[a]	1993
Bottom 20 percent	5.8	7.3	5.7	5.1	7.0	7.4 (4.5)	7.5
Second quintile	13.6	12.3	11.2	11.0	12.0	12.3 (10.4)	13.0
Third quintile	15.5	16.3	15.4	16.0	16.3	16.3 (16.0)	17.3
Fourth quintile	23.3	22.5	22.4	22.6	22.0	21.8 (22.4)	22.9
Top 20 percent	41.8	41.6	45.3	45.3	42.7	42.2 (46.7)	39.3
Gini coefficient	0.344	0.332	0.391	0.389	0.345	0.336 (0.40)	0.310

[a]Numbers in parentheses represent Korea Development Institute estimate reported in D. Leipziger et al. *The Distribution of Income and Wealth in Korea*, EDI Development Studies (Washington, D.C.: World Bank, 1992).

Sources: 1965, 1970, 1976: H. Choo, *Estimation of Size Distribution of Income and Its Sources of Change in Korea, 1982*, KDI Working Paper 8515 (Seoul: KDI, 1985). 1980, 1985, 1988, 1993: Economic Planning Board estimates as reported in National Statistics Office, *Social Statistics Summary* (Seoul: NSO, various years).

there is little evidence that the 1980s witnessed any deterioration in the distribution of income.[5]

Something else is missing. One source of the inequality that fueled labor's anger, and one not adequately captured in any of the surveys just described, was growing inequality in the distribution of wealth. Unrealized increases in capital gains, from holding financial or real assets, do not show up in conventional estimates of household income but represent potentially significant sources of inequality in the command over resources. In one of the few detailed studies of the distribution of wealth in Korea, Leipziger et al. conclude that "considerable wealth [became] concentrated in the hands *of the top 1 percent* of the population—almost exclusively through landownership" (emphasis added). The top 1 percent owned 44 percent of total land value in 1988; the top 10 percent, 77 percent. Land values between 1974 and 1989 appreciated at an estimated rate that was three times as fast as real gross national product (GNP) and in some years the resulting capital gains exceeded total GNP growth.[6] These increases in wealth were enormous, and they were concentrated in few hands.

The average Korean worker viewed this accumulation of wealth, with the benefits of economic growth mostly accruing to the privileged few, as unfair. The average worker, by comparison, had little or no wealth, in either land or financial assets. Instead, he had experienced housing prices that had escalated faster than the overall consumer price index and perceived a widening gap between his own circumstances and those of greater economic means.

The perspective of the average worker is understandable, but do the trends in the distribution of wealth warrant a reversal of the assessment that Korea was a case of shared growth? Do trends in the distribution of wealth overwhelm those reported for the distribution of income? These are empirical questions that are not easy to answer precisely. Mapping changes in the distribution of wealth into changes in the distribution of income is not straightforward and is not commonly done for any economy. Because wealth tends to consist of unrealized capital gains, it is difficult to know how to evaluate these gains as an element of a changing distribution of income.

Ideally, we want to know the expected flow of income these assets would generate over time. At a minimum, this flow would be far lower than the unrealized capital gain in asset values, since the gain would have to be distributed over a period of time. A second problem is that estimates of capital gains to land or other assets refer to prices at the margin. If all landowners attempted to capitalize their assets, the average price would be lower and the impact correspondingly less on any imputed element of the distribution of income.

The distribution of wealth in Korea, as in all other countries, is more unequally distributed than is income. The distribution of wealth also became significantly more unequal in the 1970s and 1980s and independently contributed to the dissatisfaction with economic outcomes expressed by many Koreans. The trend in the wealth distribution suggests that the distribution of income, if the permanent income flow from unrealized capital gains were included, became more unequal than is conventionally reported. However, the magnitude of this change would be nowhere near as large as the reported concentration of wealth, nor need it overwhelm Korea's success in maintaining relative income equality. The conclusion remains that the vast majority of Korean households were partners in and beneficiaries of the growth of their economy.

The Scope of This Book

A lack of political freedoms and growing inequality in the distribution of wealth fueled popular discontent in Korea, but there were other economic grievances and reasons for dissatisfaction. To begin the analysis of some of these other causes, Chapter 2, by Lim Hy-Sop, presents an overview of class formation during the course of Korean industrialization. Lim reviews sociological research on Korea that documents the nation's rapid evolution from an essentially classless society in the early 1960s to the differentiated class structure of the contemporary period. Whereas the precise definition and determinants of social classes vary according to different authors, Lim makes clear the remarkable transformation of Korea's rural peasant society into a world of capitalist, farming, and working classes. That the rapid transformation of an essentially equal and homogeneous society should produce significant social tensions is no surprise, and Lim presents the survey research data that document the locus and depth of dissatisfaction reported by various groups.

Lim concludes that Korea's differentiated class structure, coupled with the evolution of new social forces, demand reform of the prevailing political and economic system in the direction of decentralization, pluralization, and democratization. Reforms are required to resolve the inherent contradictions between the concentrated and centralized systems of the past and the highly differentiated social system of the present.

Chapters 3 through 6 focus on Korean labor as a distinct social and economic group. The analysis begins by asking how economic growth has benefited Korean workers. This approach is different from that employed in previous discussions of Korea's labor market, where the focus has been largely on the reverse: labor's contribution to growth. Often mentioned in such studies is the pivotal role played by a highly educated and industrious workforce. Low wages and long hours are cited as critical to the record of superior export performance. Others call attention to the contribution to growth of a "free" labor market, one, at least until recently, "unfettered" by unions and unconstrained by "pro-labor" legislation such as minimum wage statutes.[7]

Although much remains to be understood about the relationship between Korea's labor market and rapid economic growth, far less has been documented about the consequences of economic growth for Korean workers. With a little bit of digging, one finds two views on the nation's labor market experience. The conventional argument emphasizes continuously low levels of recorded unemployment, generally low levels of labor unrest, and rapid expansion of well-paying jobs. The frequently cited statistics include real wage gains that for twenty-five years averaged over 8 percent per annum accompanied by employment growth of similar magnitude. Rapid growth in well-paying jobs helped to maintain a distribution of income that is among the world's most equal.

But there is also a dark side to Korea's labor market experience, one raised primarily by opposition leaders, journalists, and scholars of a more radical bent.[8] The statistics on labor market expansion may not be disputed by these authors, but they take issue with the representativeness of reported benefits, as well as with various other dimensions of the quality of Korean working life. Specifically, international data suggest that Korea maintained the longest workweek in manufacturing of any other developed or developing country. Rates of industrial accidents and fatalities are alleged to have been among the world's highest, as was the level of wage discrimination against Korean women. Korean workers have had, again by international standards, rather limited rights to organize freely and engage in collective bargaining and more generally did not enjoy due process under the law in the handling of grievances both large and small. For those who focus on the dark side, the explosion of labor unrest in 1987 stands as evidence that wage and employment gains were not enough to satisfy the needs and aspirations of Korea's expanding industrial workforce.

The true character of the Korean labor market experience includes elements of both the bright and dark sides. One objective of this book is to assess these elements more fully. We seek to offer a better understanding of the economic determinants of worker grievances, especially with regard to the distribution of wage rewards and the quality of working life; contribute to an accurate assessment of Korea's record of growth with equality through the analysis of distributional trends in wages; and provide a more complete characterization of how the Korean labor market operates.

Chapter 3, by David Lindauer, focuses on the transformation of Korea's labor force from predominantly agricultural to industrial pursuits. The analysis of nonagricultural employment occupies all subsequent discussion until Chapter 7. Restricting the focus to the performance of the formal sector within manufacturing, real wage gains and employment expansion in Korea are placed in an international perspective. Relationships between the growth of employment and real wages, from approximately 1965 to 1986, are presented for a group of successful middle-income economies. These international data provide a frame of reference for evaluating Korea's outstanding record of generating jobs and increasing wages.

An assessment of the full returns to Korean labor from economic growth requires going beyond the trend in average real earnings to consideration of the distribution of wage rewards. The evaluation of any growth experience will differ according to what lies behind the average— whether the majority approach the mean or whether an elite few have garnered a disproportionate share. Joung-Woo Lee and David Lindauer undertake the required distributional analysis in Chapter 4. They ask whether Korea's industrialization has been characterized by gains disproportionately accruing to workers with particular attributes or whether the gains have been widely shared.

Lee and Lindauer conclude that in absolute terms Korea's workers— male and female, educated and uneducated, in large organizations and small—made tremendous material gains over the course of rapid national economic growth. There is also considerable evidence of increasing equality of relative pay. This finding takes on added significance in the light of the tremendous expansion of employment in the wage sector in the twenty years leading up to the labor disturbances of the 1980s. Not only did workers move toward a more equal sharing of labor income, but labor income proceeded to represent larger percentages of total income.

The increasing equality of wages, however, is a statement about trends, not levels. And it is the level of wage inequality, even after a decade or more of narrowing, that continued to differentiate Korea's wage structure from that of other economies. The persistence of an unequal pay structure contributed to the perception of relative deprivation voiced by Korean workers.

An assessment of the benefits Korean labor received from several decades of rapid economic growth naturally focuses on pay and employment trends, but it must also consider the overall quality of working life. Hours worked, job safety, labor representation, and opportunities for skill development are job attributes that matter to workers. Factors responsible for rapid increases in pay or employment may not generate improvements in these other dimensions of working life.

In Chapter 5, Lee and Lindauer examine Korea's record in humanizing factory life. Specifically, they investigate some objective elements of the quality of working life—hours and industrial safety—as well as the more subjective area of job satisfaction. They conclude that Korea's weak record on nonpecuniary aspects of working life stands in sharp contrast to the high marks Korea receives on real earnings and employment growth and the movement toward a more equal distribution of labor income. These contradictory outcomes are not a paradox. Korean labor benefited most in those areas where competitive forces could successfully be relied on. Korea's industrial strategy generated a rapidly growing derived demand for labor that was a necessary condition for rapid wage and employment growth. But along other dimensions of working life, competitive forces were not enough to ensure adequate, let alone superior, performance.

Chapter 6, by Ezra Vogel and David Lindauer, adopts a more qualitative approach in its assessment of the labor unrest that exploded in Korea in the summer of 1987. Based on an intensive series of interviews with Korean labor leaders, senior managers, and government officials, the authors explore the social, economic, and political forces that first sustained and later undermined the pre-1987 labor relations system. Vogel and Lindauer argue that Korea is in the midst of a transition away from a historically repressive system of labor control. Although radical student activity played a role in the unrest that began in June 1987, the authors caution that catalysts must be distinguished from the underlying causes of social change.

Vogel and Lindauer believe that a new social compact among workers, management, and government requires dealing with broader issues of wealth distribution and political legitimacy and erecting a new framework for resolving issues directly affecting labor-management relations. Permitting labor to have a free and independent voice is central to this process, as is revision of labor laws and enforcement practices.

Jong-Gie Kim and Jae-Young Son turn their attention in Chapter 7 toward a different source of tension in Korea: rural-urban disparities and the general problem of regional development. They document the massive spatial transformation that accompanied Korean economic growth. Data on the urban-rural income gap reveal that the incomes of rural households generally kept pace with those of their urban counterparts. Although migration provided a key response mechanism to uneven regional development, broad measures of social and economic infrastructure suggest a growing gap between cities and the countryside. Not only did urban dwellers enjoy more amenities, but the opportunities for future development continued to favor the cities, especially those along the Seoul-Pusan axis. Kim and Son conclude that these outcomes were as much a result of government policies as they were of market forces.

In Chapter 8, David Lindauer summarizes the evidence on the consequences of rapid economic growth for particular groups in Korean society, especially labor. He speculates about why so many Koreans apparently were dissatisfied with their economic situations. At issue are the legitimacy of specific economic grievances and the expectations and perceptions of the Korean people. Lindauer hypothesizes that rapid growth itself, as well as a high level of intolerance for inequality in Korea, contributed to discontent. Chapter 9 offers a brief epilogue on labor outcomes and labor relations in the 1990s.

The strains that accompanied rapid growth in Korea should not come as a total surprise; after all, economic growth is an inherently uneven and unbalanced process. Nevertheless, there are lessons to be learned from Korea's experience that should be valuable to future policymakers in both Seoul and the capitals of other nations striving to emulate Korea's economic success.

NOTES

1. See J. W. Bennett and S. B. Levine, "Industrialization and Social Deprivation: Welfare, Environment, and the Postindustrial Society in Japan," in H. Patrick, ed., *Japanese Industrialization and Its Social Consequences* (Berkeley: University of California Press, 1976).
2. In a well-known article, A. O. Hirschman argues that a society's tolerance for income inequality can change over the course of economic development. His analogy, referred to as the tunnel effect, is as follows: "Suppose that I drive through a two-lane tunnel, both lanes going in the

same direction, and run into a serious traffic jam. No car moves in either lane as far as I can see (which is not very far). I am in the left lane and feel dejected. After a while the cars in the right lane begin to move. Naturally, my spirits lift considerably, for I know that the jam has been broken and that my lane's turn to move will surely come any moment now. Even though I still sit still, I feel much better off than before because of the expectation that I shall soon be on the move. But suppose that the expectation is disappointed and only the right lane keeps moving: in that case I, along with my left lane cosufferers, shall suspect foul play, and many of us will at some point become quite furious and ready to correct manifest injustice by taking direct action." A. O. Hirschman, "The Changing Tolerance for Income Inequality in the Course of Economic Development," *Quarterly Journal of Economics* 87 (November 1973): 544–565.

3. Han Sung-Joo and Park Yung-Chul, "South Korea: Democratization at Last," in James Morley, ed., *Driven by Growth: Political Change in the Asia-Pacific Region* (Armonk, N.Y.: M. E. Sharpe, 1993), pp. 163–191.

4. On June 29, 1987, Roh Tae-Woo, then the ruling Democratic Justice party's candidate to succeed President Chun Doo Hwan, announced his support for a popular election to determine the next president of the republic. This pledge set the stage for the freest national elections in Korea's history.

5. See D. Leipziger et al., *The Distribution of Income and Wealth in Korea*, EDI Development Studies (Washington, D.C.: World Bank, 1992), chap. 1.

6. Ibid., pp. 44–46, 53.

7. The contribution of human capital as a precondition for rapid growth is well articulated by Edward S. Mason et al., *The Economic and Social Modernization of the Republic of Korea: Studies in the Modernization of the Republic of Korea, 1945–1975* (Cambridge: Harvard University Press, 1980), and by R. Dornbusch and Y. C. Park, *Korean Growth Policy, Brookings Papers on Economic Activity*, vol. 2 (Washington, D.C.: Brookings, 1987). The importance of a "free" labor market in Korea is argued, for example, by Gary S. Fields, "Industrialization and Employment in Hong Kong, Korea, Singapore, and Taiwan," in Walter Galenson, ed., *Foreign Trade and Investment: Economic Growth in the Newly Industrializing Asian Countries* (Madison: University of Wisconsin Press, 1985), and Paul Kuznets, "An East Asian Model of Economic Development: Japan, Taiwan, and South Korea," *Economic Development and Cultural Change*, 36, no. 3 (Supplement) (April 1988).

8. See Kim Dae-Jung, "Korea's Labor Relations Policy," *Korean-American Relations Review*, no. 2 (1984). English-language journalists who have reported on the poor quality of working conditions in Korea include Mark Clifford, "Labour Strikes Out," *Far Eastern Economic Review,* August 27, 1987, and Susan Chira, "In Korean Factory, a Dream Is Reduced to Ashes," *New York Times,* April 6, 1988. Strong criticism of policies toward labor organizations can be found in J. West, "Review Essay: The Suboptimal 'Miracle' of South Korean State Capitalism," *Bulletin of Concerned Asian Scholars* 19, no. 3 (1987), and Asia Watch Committee, "Labor," *Human Rights in Korea* (New York: Asia Watch Committee, 1986). Also see Frederic Deyo, *Beneath the Miracle: Labor Subordination in the New Asian Industrialism* (Berkeley: University of California Press, 1989), aptly titled, and Ronald Rogers, "An Exclusionary Labor Regime Under Pressure: The Changes in Labor Relations in the Republic of Korea Since Mid-1989," *UCLA Pacific Basin Law Journal* 8, no. 1 (Spring 1990). A mainstream account of Korea's labor market experience appears in Alice Amsden, *Asia's Next Giant: South Korea and Late Industrialization* (New York: Oxford University Press, 1989), chap. 8.

2

The Evolution of Social Classes and Changing Social Attitudes

Hy-Sop Lim

In the past three decades, industrialization has transformed Korea from an agrarian into an urbanized industrial society. In 1963, primary industry (agriculture, forestry, and fishing) produced 40 percent of the gross national product (GNP), while the share of secondary industry (manufacturing, mining, construction, and utilities) remained a mere 14 percent. After two decades the relative weights of the two industries had reversed, with secondary industry producing 35 percent and primary industry contributing only 18 percent by 1983. This rapid shift to an industrial structure has helped the Korean economy develop, but it has also caused profound changes in the social structure and values of the Korean people.

The social class system before the 1960s was a relatively undifferentiated one, since farming families made up approximately two-thirds of the total population. The remaining third of the population belonged to other social classes: the old middle class or petite bourgeoisie (about 13 percent of the population), the new middle class (7 percent), industrial workers (9 percent), and the urban lower class (6 percent).[1] Moreover, the traditional landowner class disintegrated as a result of the land reform of 1949, but a new capitalist class had not yet emerged. Thus, Korean society in the early 1960s was fairly homogeneous, characterized by considerable equality in class status and income.

Throughout the 1960s and into the 1970s most Koreans, regardless of class background, focused on improving their own family status through hard work and educating their children, and they were less concerned with social and political issues such as democratization or a more equal distribution of national income and wealth. A survey of intellectuals (professors and journalists) in 1972 reported that respondents listed the most important goals of national development in the following order: industrialization (29 percent), improvement in the standard of living (23 percent), growth of the middle class (15 percent), rationalization of way of life (13 percent), and political democratization (6 percent).[2] Starting in the 1970s public concern about political development and fair distribution gradually increased.

Public sentiments began to change for several reasons. During the 1970s President Park Chung Hee initiated his "Revitalization Revolution" and added a constitutional amendment that made him president for life, strengthening his authoritarian rule. This political scheme to extend his presidency reawakened people's concern about political democratization and sparked an antigovernment movement. Over the same period, Korea's middle class, strongly committed to liberal democracy as a consequence of high economic growth, increased to nearly half the total population. Economic disparities between social classes and regions also were on the rise, and a sense of relative deprivation became widely diffused among the general population. As the social class structure became more differentiated, people became more aware of their own class interests.

The dynamics of the economic, political, and social development of Korean society in the past thirty years cannot be fully understood without an analysis of changes in social structures and values. This chapter analyzes the social class system and social attitudes of contemporary Korean society and discusses the policy implications that follow.

Changes in Social Class Structure

Differentiation of Social Classes

A number of sociologists have analyzed the social class system of contemporary Korean society since the 1960s from different theoretical perspectives. Suh Kwan-Mo presented a "polarization model" or "two-classes, three-strata model" of a class system from a basically Marxist theoretical perspective. According to his analysis of the economically active population, two basic social classes, capitalists and the working class, have grown considerably. At the same time, the population shares of intermediate social strata such as the salaried middle, the intelligentsia, and the self-employed have gradually decreased as industrialization has proceeded. The size of the capitalist class increased from 0.4 percent of the total population in 1960 to 1.1 percent in 1980, and the proportion of the working-class population expanded from 32 percent in 1960 to 45 percent in 1980, as the proportion of those in the intermediate strata decreased from 68 percent to 54 percent (Table 2-1). Suh's analysis indicates that the social class system of Korean society became somewhat polarized during this period.[3] A somewhat similar analysis, presented by Kim Young-Mo in 1982, also indicates that the capitalist and working classes have grown significantly and the "old middle stratum" has rapidly declined, while the "new middle stratum" has grown (Table 2-2).[4]

Unlike Suh and Kim, who used employment status as a basic criterion of class categorization, Hong Doo-Seung analyzed the class system of contemporary Korean society from a Weberian perspective, taking level of control over social resources (means of production, wealth, power, education, etc.) as a determinant of social class. He also introduced the concept of sectors, which he identified as the organizational, agricultural, and self-employed sectors. He insisted that the capitalist economic system in Korea is still developing, and thus a substantial proportion of the

Table 2-1.   Suh Kwan-Mo's Analysis of Social Class Structure (percentages)

	1960	1970	1975	1980
Capitalist class	0.4	0.5	0.9	1.1
Intermediary strata	65.8	64.5	58.5	54.3
Salaried middle stratum (managers)	0.9	1.1	1.5	2.1
Intelligentsia	2.0	2.6	3.0	3.6
Self-employed	64.9	61.4	54.0	48.5
Small business owners	10.1	13.3	14.5	16.8
Independent farmers	54.8	48.1	39.4	31.7
Working class	31.7	34.4	40.6	44.7
Clerical workers	1.9	4.5	5.6	7.2
Sales workers	0.6	1.9	2.3	2.4
Service workers	3.7	4.5	4.5	4.0
Industrial workers	9.7	17.0	21.6	24.0
Farm laborers	8.1	2.3	2.3	1.3
Unemployed	7.7	4.2	4.3	5.8

Source: Economic Planning Board (EPB), Sample Surveys of Economically Active Population: 1955–1980, Suh Kwan-Mo, *Class Composition and Class Differentiation of Contemporary Korean Society* (Seoul: Han-Ul, 1984), pp. 95–97.

Table 2-2.   Kim Young-Mo's Analysis of Social Class Structure (percentages)

Classes	1960	1966	1970	1975	1980
Capitalist class	1.7	0.7	2.4	2.9	3.7
Old middle stratum	65.6	55.4	47.9	39.1	35.8
New middle stratum	6.8	9.3	13.5	14.5	17.3
Working class	24.7	34.6	35.5	43.3	43.3
Unknown	1.2	—	0.7	—	—

Source: EPB, Sample Surveys of Economically Active Population: 1955–1980; Kim Young-Mo, *A Study of Social Stratification in Contemporary Korea* (Seoul: Il-Chokak, 1982), p. 383.

economically active population remains in the self-employed and agricultural sectors. Hong identified seven different social classes from the three sectors (Table 2-3).[5]

According to Hong's analysis of change in the social class system between 1960 and 1980, the relatively homogeneous and simple class system of the early 1960s was transformed into a highly differentiated one by the 1980s. In 1960, the farmers' class (independent farmers and rural lower classes combined) composed 64 percent of the total population, and other social classes were relatively undifferentiated.[6] By 1980, however, the old middle class, new middle class, working class, and independent farmers' class had become equivalent social forces in terms of population. As shown in Table 2-3, each of those four social classes constituted approximately 20 percent of the total population. Between 1960 and 1980, the populations of the old middle, new middle, and working classes grew substantially, and the farmers' and marginal lower class populations decreased considerably. Thus, Hong asserts, the social class system of contemporary Korea has become a relatively differentiated one in which several different social forces are in competition with one another for their respective class interests.

Koo Hagen adopted, with some revision, Wright's class model to analyze the social class system of Korea. He classified six social classes, then concluded that the working class had grown the fastest of all class categories and as early as the late 1970s had become the largest social class, with the exception of farmers (Table 2-4). He noted that the relative size of the middle class (new middle class and petite bourgeoisie) had increased only slightly and thus remained relatively stable during the early stage of industrialization. This differs from Hong's analysis, in which both the old and new middle classes are shown to have grown considerably.[7]

Table 2-3. Hong Doo-Seung's Analysis of Social Class Structure (percentages)

Social Classes	1960	1970	1975	1980
Upper class	0.9	1.3	1.2	1.8
New middle class	6.6	14.2	15.7	17.7
Old middle class	13.0	14.8	14.5	20.8
Working class	8.9	16.9	19.9	22.6
Urban lower class	6.6	8.0	7.5	5.9
Independent farmers' class	40.0	28.0	28.2	23.2
Rural lower class	24.0	16.7	12.9	8.1

Source: EPB, Sample Surveys of Economically Active Population: 1955–1980, and analysis of 1 percent sample of the 1975 census; Hong Doo-Seung, "A Study of Social Stratification Through the Analysis of Occupational Structure," *Social Science and Policy Studies* 5, no. 3 (1983).

Table 2-4. Koo Hagen's Analysis of Social Class Structure, 1960–1975 (percentages)

Classes	1960	1966	1970	1975
Capitalist class	0.7	0.9	1.0	0.8
New middle class	8.6	8.6	9.5	10.5
Petite bourgeoisie	5.6	10.3	6.3	6.8
Working class	8.7	12.4	19.2	21.1
Marginal class	10.2	11.0	12.8	11.5
Farmers' class	66.2	56.8	51.2	49.2

Source: Koo Hagen, "A Preliminary Analysis of Social Class Structure of Contemporary Korean Society," *Reinterpretation of Korean Society* 1 (1985).

The different results of these various studies are due mostly to the different definitions of class categories employed by the analysts (see Appendix 2A for definitions of the social classes), since all of their analyses were based on the same data sources. All four analysts used Census Reports and Sample Surveys of the Economically Active Population, compiled and published officially by the Economic Planning Board.[8] They also made use of other official statistics and their own sample surveys, but only for supplementary analytical purposes.

The most important disagreement among these analyses pertains to the trend of the middle class. Suh and Kim showed a general decline of the middle class, attributed to a rapid decrease in the population of the old middle class or petite bourgeoisie. In contrast, Hong showed that the relative size of the middle class had grown considerably, and Koo reached the conclusion that the new middle class and petite bourgeoisie had remained relatively stable. This disagreement is largely due to differences in these analysts' definitions of the old middle class and petite bourgeoisie. Suh and Kim included self-employed independent farmers in the category of the old middle stratum or intermediary stratum, and Hong and Koo made a separate category for the farmers' class.

Except for disagreement about the trend and the fate of the middle class, the analysts seem to agree in their assessments of general trends in social class transformation during the past decades. First, all four conclude that social classes in the modern, organizational sector, such as the capitalist, the new middle, and the working classes, grew considerably, while the social classes that belong to the traditional (agricultural and informal) sectors failed to retain their relative population sizes. Second, all analyses reached the conclusion that the social class system of Korea has become much more differentiated and complex than that of the early 1960s.

Growth of the Capitalist Class and Concentration of Economic Power and Wealth

The upper or ruling class in Korea today consists of large business owners or capitalists, holders of senior management posts in the government and private companies, and political elites. During the past decades of industrialization, the population of the upper class has increased from about 1 percent to 2 percent, as shown in Table 2-3. More important, economic power and wealth are highly concentrated in the upper class as a consequence of the government's growth-first economic development policies.

A 1989 analysis reports that the thirty largest corporate groups, comprising less than 19 percent of the manufacturing firms in Korea, were responsible for 40 percent of gross output, 33 percent of value added, 40 percent of fixed assets, and 18 percent of employment in 1985. The largest five corporate groups were responsible for 23 percent of gross output, 19 percent of value added, 20 percent of fixed assets, and 10 percent of employment in the manufacturing industry, indicating a high degree of economic concentration (Table 2-5).[9]

Another analysis revealed that the proportion of small and medium-sized firms in manufacturing decreased in number from 99 percent in 1960 to 95 percent in 1980, in employment from 76 percent to 45 percent, and in value added from 66 percent to 28 percent (Table 2-6).[10] Concentration of economic power also brought about the concentration of wealth. More than two-thirds of private land (excluding farmland) was owned by 5 percent of all land owners or 3 percent of the richest segment of the economically active population.[11] Concentration of economic power resulted mainly from the export-led, growth-first economic policies of the previous governments in which large businesses were given

Table 2-5. Concentration of Economic Power in Manufacturing Industry

Corporate Groups	Number of Corpora- tions within Groups	% of Total Employ- ment	% of Gross Output	% of Value Added	% of Fixed Assets
5 largest groups	94	9.7	23.0	18.7	20.4
10 largest groups	147	11.7	30.2	24.2	27.9
15 largest groups	190	14.4	33.9	27.3	31.6
20 largest groups	218	15.5	36.4	29.5	34.4
25 largest groups	246	16.6	38.5	31.4	36.8
30 largest groups	270	17.6	40.2	33.1	39.6

Source: Lee Kyu-Eok, "Causes of and Policies on Concentration of Economic Power," *Shinpyoung Forum* (May 1989): 8.

Table 2-6. Relative Weight of Medium and Small-Sized Firms in Manufacturing Industry (percentages)

Size of Corporations by Number of Employees	Number of Corporations		Employment		Value Added	
	1960	1982	1960	1982	1960	1982
5–19	81.3	62.7	30.9	10.9	28.6	4.7
20–49	13.2	18.8	22.3	10.5	18.4	5.8
50–99	3.1	9.1	11.4	11.2	9.9	7.6
100–199	1.5	5.0	11.4	12.2	9.4	9.9
200–499	0.7	3.2	10.7	16.6	15.8	17.0
500 or more	0.2	1.6	13.2	38.6	17.7	55.0
Large-scale corporations	0.9	4.7	23.9	55.2	33.5	72.0
Medium or small-sized firms	99.1	95.4	76.1	44.8	66.5	28.0

Note: Large-scale corporations are defined as those with more than two hundred employees.

Source: Korea Industrial Bank, Census of Mining and Manufacturing Industry, 1960–1982, quoted from Lee Dae-Keun, "Economic Growth and Structural Disequilibrium," in Korean Social Science Research Council, ed., *Social Change and Problems* (Seoul: Bum-Mun Sa, 1986), p.194.

special benefits and support from the government. As a result, the upper capitalist class has been the most privileged social class since industrialization began, and it has become the most powerful social class in terms of its capacity to control social resources.

Expansion of the Middle Class

As a consequence of industrialization and economic development during the past thirty years, both old and new middle classes have grown rapidly as politically influential social forces. The old middle class, defined as self-employed small businessmen, grew from 13 percent of the population in 1960 to 21 percent in 1980. This class has gained population from the farmers' class, some members of which changed their occupation from farming to small business in urban areas, though it lost some members to the new middle class. The quantitative growth of the old middle class was due to the rapid increase of small business owners in the service sector as the rate of urbanization surpassed that of industrialization.

Members of the old middle class benefited from economic development, since most of them achieved upward social mobility, in spite of their relatively low level of education, through occupational mobility from farming to self-employed small businesses in sales, service, or manufacturing industries. More recently, they have become increasingly frustrated with and critical of economic concentration.

The new middle class also grew rapidly through the expansion of private industries during the age of industrialization. New members of this class were recruited mainly from the children of the farmers' class who received higher education. Thus, most of them experienced inter-generational class mobility through the channel of college education. The number of college students has increased more than forty times since the liberation of the country, and most college graduates have been absorbed into the expanding new middle class.

As a result, the population share of the middle class increased from 20 percent in 1960 to 39 percent in 1980, and it is still growing. Moreover, the proportion of the population that subjectively identifies itself with the middle class also increased, exceeding 60 percent. Furthermore, middle-class members are among the most educated and politically active people. In this sense, Korean society can be said to have become a middle-class society and is becoming more so as the proportion of the middle-class population continues to increase.

Emergence of the Working Class as a New Social Force

In the early 1960s, the working-class population did not exceed 10 percent of the total population. As industrialization progressed, the population of this class gradually expanded and reached 22 percent by 1980 (see Table 2-3). Mostly young, unmarried, and relatively less educated workers with rural backgrounds were recruited by the fast-growing and labor-intensive manufacturing industry. These workers were more concerned with improving their families' economic conditions than with altering their poor working conditions, which were characterized by low wages, extended work hours, and an unpleasant and sometimes hazardous work environment. The work ethic of Korean industrial workers, characterized by diligence and high motivation, is well documented by numerous studies.[12]

As manufacturing grew rapidly and the number of industrial workers increased, workers in large manufacturing firms gradually became more active in organizing and participating in labor unions. As shown in Table 2-7, the number of unionized workers increased from 302,000 in 1965 to 1.7 million by 1983. However, the proportion of unionized workers among total industrial labor remained at approximately 20 percent throughout the 1970s. It declined to 15 percent in the 1980s due to labor law reform in 1980 that introduced repressive measures to discourage organization of labor unions and labor disputes. In spite of such repressive labor laws and government labor policies, an average of a hundred cases of virtually illegal labor disputes occurred every year

Table 2-7. Number and Proportion of Unionized Workers, 1965–1985

Year	Employees (in 1,000 persons)	Unionized Employees (in 1,000 persons)	Proportion of Unionized Employees (%)
1965	1,347	302	22.4
1970	2,363	473	20.0
1971	2,520	497	19.7
1972	2,529	515	20.4
1973	2,683	548	20.4
1974	2,974	656	22.1
1975	3,258	750	23.0
1976	3,630	846	23.3
1977	3,922	955	24.3
1978	4,389	1,055	24.0
1979	4,609	1,088	23.6
1980	4,728	948	20.1
1981	4,946	967	19.6
1982	5,160	984	19.1
1983	5,594	1,010	18.1
1984	6,031	1,011	16.8
1985	6,397	1,004	15.7
1986	6,666	1,036	15.5
1987	7,315	1,267	17.3
1988	7,771	1,707	22.0

Source: EPB, *Social Indicators in Korea* (1989), p. 146.

during the 1970s and 1980s.[13] Such a rapid increase in industrial workers and union membership and continuous labor disputes even under repressive labor laws reflects that the working class has grown as a significant social and political force in contemporary Korean society.

Farmers: A Relatively Disadvantaged Class

The independent farmers' class, comprising nearly half of the total population in early 1960, has shrunk to only one-fifth, although its contribution to economic development and industrialization has remained constant. The farmers' class supplied an abundant labor force of mostly young and highly motivated workers to the fast-growing manufacturing and service industries. Farmers invested a substantial portion of their family income in the education of their children, who were recruited as white- or blue-collar workers for the urban industrial sectors. Some farmers moved to the cities themselves and became self-employed small businessmen, while others remained in their rural villages to cultivate and supply food to industrial workers.

Members of the farmers' class, who cultivated farmland and produced agricultural products as their ancestors had for generations, suffered from relatively low growth in the agricultural sector in comparison with the urban manufacturing and service industries. The average annual income of farm households was lower than that of urban industrial workers for most of the 1960s, 1970s, and 1980s. In that sense, the independent farmers' class has been relatively disadvantaged over the course of industrialization.

Resolution of Absolute Poverty in the Marginal Lower Class

When the Korean War ended in 1953, a large proportion of the population was left in a condition of absolute poverty. One analysis reported that 41 percent of the total population in 1965 consisted of families in absolute poverty.[14] This level was reduced to less than 10 percent in 1980 as the Korean economy flourished. By the late 1980s approximately two million people, or about 5 percent of the total population, were supported by government public assistance programs; most of them belonged to families in which bread earners were absent, aged, disabled, or unemployed due to ill health or a lack of skills.

Other low-income families, such as day laborers, street peddlers, and farm laborers also belong to the marginal lower class. According to Hong's analysis, the population of the urban and rural lower classes amounts to 14 percent of the total population.[15] (See Table 2-5.) This class is alienated from the benefits of economic growth and industrialization in that its members have failed to escape from poverty by their own means, as most other Koreans have succeeded in improving their standard of living and family status during the period of high economic growth.

Changes in Social Values and Attitudes

The changes in the social class system inevitably brought changes in social consciousness, values, and attitudes. People of different classes developed diverse social attitudes, depending on their economic and social advancement, deprivation, or alienation during the period of industrialization.

Despite most Koreans' having experienced improvements in their economic and social conditions and, to some extent, upward intergenerational mobility through education or occupational mobility, a sense of relative deprivation or social inequality seems to have increased gradually. This sense has become widely diffused among the classes, owing to rapidly rising expectations and widening economic disparities between social classes and regions. Moreover, as the social class system has become more differentiated, class consciousness among the general population has also developed in the sense that people are now more aware of their class interests than before. Class consciousness among contemporary Koreans, however, has not developed to the extent of class antagonism, though some radical ideologues insist that class struggle is coming in Korean society.

Most Koreans, including workers, farmers, and the poor, still believe that opportunities for social mobility are open to them as long as they work hard. They are generally optimistic about their future since they believe the economy continues to develop and grow. Moreover, a majority of Koreans already have a middle-class consciousness through which they identify themselves with the middle class rather than the lower or working classes.

It is equally true that the majority of contemporary Koreans are not content with income disparities or with the distribution of wealth and the high degree of economic concentration. The majority has demanded strong political, social, and economic reforms designed to democratize their society further.

Class Consciousness

Most Koreans identify their own and others' class status on the basis of control over social resources such as income, property, education, occupational prestige, and family background, as well as in terms of position in productive relations, such as employment status and type of work. This multidimensional class consciousness is demonstrated by a relatively high level of middle-class consciousness among all occupational groups, including farmers and industrial workers (Table 2-8).[16] For instance, although 72 percent of industrial workers designate their social class as working class, 17 percent categorize themselves as old middle class. And 45 percent of farmers identify their class status as old middle class, while only 38 percent insist they belong to the working class. As a whole, more than half the respondents believe they belong to either the old or the new middle class.

Other surveys on subjective class consciousness consistently report that approximately 60 percent of the population has a middle-class identity.[17] In a survey conducted by the National Bureau of Statistics, 61 percent of the national sample classified themselves as middle class, and 40 percent identified their own class status as lower class (Table 2-9).[18] This widely shared middle-class consciousness can be attributed to improvements in the living standards, educational attainment, and upward social mobility that a broad range of people have experienced.

Table 2-8. Self-Identified Subjective Social Classes by Occupational Group, 1987 (percentages)

Occupational Group	Capitalist Class	Old Middle Class	New Middle Class	Working Class	Others
Professionals	1.0	23.3	34.4	36.4	4.4
Managers	2.6	17.3	41.6	33.3	5.2
Clerical workers	1.2	10.2	55.5	26.4	7.6
Sales	2.3	62.8	7.3	21.2	6.5
Service	2.7	49.1	10.5	31.9	5.7
Farmers	1.3	45.0	3.4	37.9	13.0
Industrial workers	0.5	17.4	6.0	72.1	3.0
Others	1.8	26.8	21.9	24.6	11.9
Total	1.7	31.1	24.5	32.6	10.1

Source: Kim Young-Mo, "Sense of Social Inequality Among Koreans," *Chung-Ang Journal of Social Sciences* 1 (1987): 20.

Table 2-9. Self-Identified Subjective Social Classes, 1988 (percentages)

Residential Area	Self-Identified Social Classes			
	Upper	Middle	Lower	Total
Urban	2.7	63.1	34.2	100.0
Rural	1.8	54.7	43.5	100.0
Total	2.4	60.6	36.9	100.0

Source: *Social Indicators in Korea*, p. 289.

A generation ago, nearly two-thirds of Koreans were either tenant farmers or simple laborers and lived in absolute poverty. Today, most of them have not only escaped from poverty but also have experienced intergenerational or career mobility. A 1989 survey reported that more than half of the national sample believed that the probability of upward mobility was high (64 percent) or moderate (30 percent) and only 6 percent of the respondents believed it was low. Chances for upward career mobility are believed to be somewhat lower than those for intergenerational mobility, but the general pattern of responses was almost identical (Table 2-10).

Sense of Relative Deprivation and Social Inequality

Nearly two-thirds of Koreans have a middle-class consciousness and believe the social class system remains open, but this does not necessarily mean that most Koreans are satisfied with their social and economic conditions. On the contrary, social discontent among the general population increased after the mid-1970s.

Table 2-10. Attitude Toward the Opportunities for Social Class Mobility, 1988 (percentages)

Type of Mobility	Possibility of Upward Mobility		
	High	Moderate	Low
Intergenerational mobility			
Urban	65.2	29.3	5.5
Rural	61.2	32.3	5.5
Total	64.0	30.2	5.8
Career mobility			
Urban	53.1	34.4	12.5
Rural	54.6	34.1	11.3
Total	53.6	34.3	12.1

Source: Ibid., p. 288.

Many sociologists contend that a sense of relative deprivation can increase during economic development if the level of expectations rises faster than the actual improvement of economic conditions. Such a sense of relative deprivation is widely diffused among Korea's middle and lower class. Sim Young-Hee classified the senses of gratification and deprivation into four categories—absolute gratification, relative gratification, absolute deprivation, and relative deprivation—according to how one evaluates one's economic condition in comparison with that of others (absolute) and with one's own position five years earlier (relative) (Figure 2-1). Sim reports that nearly half of respondents have a sense of either relative deprivation (39 percent) or absolute deprivation (9 percent) (Table 2-11), although approximately 80 percent of those surveyed believe their economic conditions have improved "about the same with others" (74 percent) or "more than others" (7 percent), and more than half of them believe their condition has improved when compared with five years ago.[19]

A sense of relative deprivation is felt more by the middle class than by the working class, and absolute deprivation is shared by more people of the old middle class than of the working class. This finding reveals that the sense of deprivation is determined more by the level of expectation than by actual economic conditions (see Figure 2-1 and Table 2-11).

Social discontent caused by a sense of relative deprivation can be intensified by a sense of social inequality, which reflects dissatisfaction with the distribution of wealth. A number of studies report that a sense of social inequality is prevalent among people of different classes. For instance, Kim Young-Mo found that more than half of the national sample (54 percent) felt they received the benefits of economic growth "less than

Figure 2-1. Sense of Gratification and Deprivation in Korea

Compared with Five Years Ago, Economic Conditions Have:			
Compared with Others	Improved	Not Changed	Worsened
Better off than others	Sense of absolute gratification	Sense of relative deprivation	Sense of absolute deprivation
About the same with others	Sense of relative gratification		
Became worse than others			

Table 2-11. Sense of Gratification and Deprivation by Social Classes (percentages)

Sense of Gratification and Deprivation	Social Class			
	New Middle Class	Old Middle Class	Working Class	All Classes
Absolute gratification	2.8	4.6	7.3	5.5
Relative gratification	46.0	37.8	50.3	47.3
Relative deprivation	44.8	38.0	35.1	38.7
Absolute deprivation	6.5	19.5	7.3	8.6

Source: Sim Young–Hee, *A Study on Relative Deprivation and Social Classes, A Research Report*

others," and approximately one-third of the respondents (36 percent) believed their share had been "about the same with others" (Table 2-12).[20] A sense of social inequality was therefore widely shared by people of different classes, though it was felt most strongly by industrial workers and farmers.

Table 2-12. Perceived Benefits of Economic Growth by Occupational Groups, 1987 (percentages)

Occupational Groups	Perceived Benefits of Economic Growth			
	More Than Others	About the Same	Less Than Others	No Answer
Professionals	12.4	38.2	48.1	0.3
Managers	11.2	38.8	51.9	—
Clerical workers	10.1	43.8	45.5	0.2
Sales	6.8	37.8	54.6	0.9
Services	8.4	36.4	54.8	0.3
Farmers	7.5	27.3	64.3	0.4
Industrial workers	6.0	20.4	73.1	0.5
Total	9.6	35.6	54.1	0.5

Source: Kim Young-Mo, "Sense of Social Inequality Among Koreans," p. 26.

Table 2-13. Opinions on the Responsibilities for Recent Militant Labor
Disputes (percentages)

Occupational Groups	Responsibilities for Labor Disputes					
	Worker	Employer	Labor Unions	Radical Move-ments	Gov't	No Answer
Professionals	4.9	57.1	5.7	7.8	23.5	0.5
Managers	5.6	55.4	8.2	11.3	17.3	1.3
Clerical workers	5.7	58.8	8.1	8.8	17.6	1.0
Sales	8.5	59.7	5.3	11.1	14.7	0.3
Services	6.6	54.3	10.5	8.7	18.4	0.9
Farmers	13.0	54.6	4.2	5.0	21.8	0.8
Industrial workers	5.0	72.6	3.5	6.0	11.9	1.0
Total	7.2	56.9	6.6	8.5	18.7	2.0

Source: Lee Hyo-Sun, "Attitudes Toward Labor Disputes," *Chung-Ang Journal of Social Sciences* 1 (1987): 77.

Attitudes Toward Labor Disputes

A sense of social inequality is based on individual perceptions that industrial workers and rural farmers have been inadequately rewarded for their contribution to economic growth. Such positions are reflected in their attitudes toward the explosive labor disputes in recent years.

A 1987 survey reports that a majority of respondents believed employers (57 percent) and the government (19 percent) were more responsible for militant labor disputes than workers themselves (7 percent) (See Table 2-13).[21] Workers are believed to have been compensated inadequately by low wage policies for too long, while employers have benefited disproportionately from the national growth-first economic policies. However, more than half the respondents were critical of the violent and illegal conduct of disputes by some labor unions and expressed concern about potentially undesirable consequences of the disputes, such as economic regression or social unrest. Another group of respondents holds the view that such labor disputes will contribute to the development of democratic patterns of industrial relations in the long run (Table 2-14).

Political Attitudes

The sense of relative deprivation and social inequality, widespread among the old and new middle classes, working class, and farmers' class, seemed to have increased recognition that a progressive party that represented and promoted the interests of disadvantaged social groups and classes was necessary in Korean politics. Korean politics historically has been characterized by ideological rigidity due to the threat of military

Table 2-14. Opinions on the Consequences of Recent Militant Labor Disputes (percentages)

Occupational Groups	Will Contribute to Democratizing Industrial Relations	Will Cause Economic Retrogression	Will Cause Social and Political Unrest	Other
Professionals	53.5	28.7	14.5	3.4
Managers	45.0	33.3	16.9	4.7
Clerical workers	53.8	28.9	15.0	2.3
Sales	43.7	34.3	17.6	4.1
Services	44.9	36.1	14.8	4.1
Farmers	36.6	39.9	15.5	7.2
Industrial workers	48.3	31.8	12.9	6.0
Total	46.9	32.9	15.6	4.6

Source: Ibid., pp. 80–81.

invasion from the North. Increasingly open attitudes among the general population toward a progressive political party therefore represents a departure from Korea's recent political history.

According to a national survey conducted in 1987, almost half of the respondents (45 percent) recognized the need for a progressive political party, and another 36 percent agreed with reservation that the North Korean threat of invasion should be eliminated before an ideologically progressive (socialist) political party is established. However, although a wide range of people recognized the need for a progressive party (Table 2-15), this does not mean that such a party receives broad support in

Table 2-15. Perceived Need for a Progressive Party in Korean Politics, 1987 (percentages)

Occupational Groups	Need of Progressive Party			
	Is Necessary	Will Be Necessary in Future	Is Unnecessary	No Answer
Professionals	46.8	38.5	12.7	1.8
Managers	39.0	41.1	16.9	2.9
Clerical workers	45.0	39.5	12.6	2.8
Sales	44.3	38.7	15.5	1.4
Services	45.6	38.3	14.8	1.2
Farmers	50.8	28.2	20.2	0.7
Industrial workers	49.7	31.8	17.9	0.5
Total	44.7	36.3	16.6	2.2

Source: Kim Min-Ha, "Korean's Political Attitudes," *Chung-Ang Journal of Social Sciences* 1 (1987): 45.

Table 2-16.   Support of Political Parties, 1987 (percentages)

Occupational Groups	Government Party	Other Conservative Opposition Parties	Progressive Party	No Answer
Professionals	20.7	56.9	7.2	15.2
Managers	27.3	51.6	6.1	15.0
Clerical workers	21.9	56.6	3.3	18.2
Sales	27.6	54.5	5.6	12.3
Services	22.3	56.2	5.1	16.4
Farmers	32.8	48.1	5.5	13.6
Industrial workers	20.9	59.4	7.0	12.7
Total	24.4	55.4	5.1	15.1

Source: Ibid., p. 49.

elections. Kim Min-Ha's survey found that the actual rate of support failed to exceed 5 percent of voters (Table 2-16).[22]

Conclusion: Policy Implications

Korean society has experienced profound and rapid social change during the past three decades of industrialization. The social class system, which was largely homogeneous until the early 1960s, has become differentiated into a number of heterogeneous social forces, such as the upper capitalist class, old middle class, new middle class, working class, and farmers' class. The evolution and growth of these divergent social classes have made contemporary Korean society complex and dynamic.

The growing middle and working classes have become more conscious of social and political issues, including democratization and the distribution of income and wealth. Social conflicts such as labor disputes are increasing, and radicals have advocated revolutionary class struggle. Most Koreans, however, are politically reform minded in the sense that they demand a more democratized political system and a more egalitarian distributive system but are generally against radical or revolutionary means. Their optimistic view of their future and the continued development of the Korean economy makes them believe that any revolutionary change in the social order is potentially detrimental to their own interests.

Social discontent is largely directed toward the excessive concentration of economic power and wealth, which people believe should be corrected by reformist economic policies and a more democratic political process. A widely shared sense of relative deprivation and social inequality is reflected in such discontent and in demands for political and economic reforms.

A differentiated social system and the evolution of new social forces or classes demand reform of the political and economic system in the direction of decentralization, pluralization, and democratization. Highly concentrated political power and economic wealth inherited from previous authoritarian governments should be redistributed and diffused among people of different classes. In this way the contradictions or disequilibrium between the pluralized and highly differentiated social system and the concentrated and centralized political and economic system can be resolved. The basic problem facing Korean society today is how political, economic, and social subsystems can be readjusted and restructured through democratic reforms without causing serious social conflict or adverse effects on economic development.

Appendix 2A: Class Models and Definitions of Social Class Categories

Suh Kwan-Mo's Two-Class, Three-Strata Model and Definitions of Class Categories

In Suh's model, only two basic social classes, the capitalists and the working class, exist in capitalist society. In transitional Korean society, however, three intermediary social strata between the basic social classes are identified. Operational definitions of class categories are as follows:

1. *The capitalist class*: Owners of means of production and the functional capitalists, defined as employers and managers of businesses and the government (section chiefs and above).
2. *The working class*: Wage-earning manual workers and non-manual clerical workers in businesses and the government, farm laborers, and the unemployed.
3. *The intermediary strata:* Three social strata: the salaried middle stratum, defined as holders of lower-level management posts (below the level of section chief) in businesses and the government; the intelligentsia, consisting of professionals and engineers and the self-employed stratum, comprising self-employed businessmen (urban petite bourgeoisie) and independent farmers (rural petite bourgeoisie).

Table 2A-1. Kim Young-Mo's Class Model and Definitions of Class Categories

Occupational Categories	Employment Status		
	Employer	Self-Employed	Employed
Professional and engineering	Capitalist class	Old middle class	New middle class
Administrative and management	Capitalist class	Old middle class	New middle class
Clerical work	Capitalist class	Old middle class	New middle class
Sales	Capitalist class	Old middle class	Working class
Services	Capitalist class	Old middle class	Working class
Agriculture	Capitalist class	Old middle class	Working class
Manufacturing and mining	Old middle class	Working class	Working class

Source: Kim Young-Mo, *A Study of Social Stratification in Contemporary Korea* (Seoul: IL-Chokak, 1982), reproduced with permission.

Kim Young-Mo's Two-Class, Two-Strata Class Model

Two basic social classes—capitalists and the working class—and two intermediary social strata—the old middle and the new middle strata—are operationally defined by occupational categories and employment status, as shown in Table 2A-1.

Hong Doo-Seung's Seven-Class Model and Definitions of Class Categories

Hong's social class categories are determined by the level of control over social resources held by each occupational category of the three different sectors (organizational, self-employment, and agricultural), as shown in Table 2A-2. The levels of control over social resources are defined in his analysis of occupations from a 1 percent sample of the 1975 census.

Table 2A-2. Hong Doo-Seung's Class Model and Definitions of Class Categories

Level of Control over Social Resources	Sector		
	Organizational	Self-Employed	Agricultural
High	Upper class	Upper class	———
Intermediate	New middle class	Old middle class	Independent
Low	Working class	Urban lower class	Rural lower

Source: Hong Doo-Seung, "Study of Social Stratification."

Table 2A-3. Koo Hagen's Class Model and Definitions of Class Categories

Class Categories	Ownership or Control of the Means of Production	Purchase or Sale of Labor Power	Manual-Nonmanual Distinction
Capitalists	Yes	Purchase	Nonmanual
New middle class	No	Sale	Nonmanual
Working class	No	Sale	Manual
Petite bourgeoisie	Yes	Self-employed	Nonmanual
Marginal class	No	Mostly self-employed	Manual

Source: Koo Hagen, "Preliminary Analysis of Social Class Structure."

Koo Hagen's Six-Class Model and Definitions of the Class Categories
Koo classified five social classes in his revised Wright's class model, as shown in Table 2A-3, but he added a farmers' class in his analysis of the social class structure of Korean society, making the number of class categories six instead of five.

NOTES

1. Social classes are defined, in this instance, according to economic sector and the level of control over social resources, following the analysis of Hong Doo-Seung, "A Study of Social Stratification through the Analysis of Occupational Structure," *Social Science and Policy Research* 5, no. 3 (1983). The old middle class refers to those who are self-employed and have an intermediate level of control over social resources. The new middle class is in the modern (organizational) sector of the economy and also has an intermediate level of control over social resources.
2. Hong Seung-Chick, *A Study on Intellectual's Value-Orientations* (Seoul: Sam-Young Sa., 1972), p. 161.
3. Suh Kwan-Mo, *Class Composition and Class Differentiation of Contemporary Korean Society* (Seoul: Han-Ul, 1984), pp. 95–97.
4. Kim Young-Mo, *A Study of Social Stratification in Korea* (Seoul: Il-Chokak, 1982), p. 328.
5. Hong Doo-Seung, "A Preliminary Analysis of Korean Social Stratification," *Tradition and Change in Korean Society* (Seoul: Bum-Mun Sa, 1983), pp. 176–179.
6. Independent farmers and the rural lower classes differ in their degree of control over social resources. The former has an intermediate level of control, the latter a low level. See Appendix 2A for further discussion.

7. See Koo Hagen and Hong Doo-Seung, "Class and Income Inequality in Korea," *American Sociological Review*, 45 (1980): 610–626 for their revision of Wright's class model, and see Koo Hagen, "Transformation of the Korean Class Structure: The Impact of Dependent Development," in Robert Robinson, *Research in Social Stratification and Mobility*, vol. 4 (Greenwich, CT: JAI Press, 1985), and Koo Hagen, "The State, Industrial Structure, and Labor Politics: Comparison of South Korea and Taiwan," Korean Sociological Association, ed., *Industrial East Asia* (1989), pp. 21–37.
8. Sample Surveys of the Economically Active Population were conducted by the Bureau of Statistics, Economic Planning Board using a 1 percent sample in 1955, 20 percent in 1960, 10 percent in 1966, 10 percent in 1970, 5 percent in 1975, and 15 percent in 1980.
9. Lee Kyu-Eok, "Causes of and Policies on the Concentration of Economic Power" (Shinpyung Forum, May 1989), 8.
10. Lee Dai-Keun, "Economic Growth and Structural Disequilibrium," in Korean Social Science Research Council, ed., *Social Change and Problems* (Seoul: Bum-Mun Sa, 1986), p. 194.
11. Hong Won-Tak, "Korean Economy at Cross-Road," *Sasang Quarterly* 1 (Summer 1989): 162–163.
12. See, for instance, Kim Kyoung-Dong, "Occupational Values and Social Structure," *Social Science and Policy Studies* 5, no. 3 (1983): 31–67; Lee Kak-Bum, "Industrial Development and Labor Market," in Korean Sociological Association, ed., *Where Korean Society Is Headed* (1983), pp. 43–59.
13. See Kim Sung-Kuk, "Industrialization and Industrial Conflict," in Korean Sociological Association, ed., *A Study of Social Conflicts in Korea* (1985), p. 198.
14. Suh Sang-Mok et al., *Current State of the Poverty and Policies on the Poor* (Seoul: Korea Development Research Institute, 1981), pp. 43–59.
15. Hong Doo-Seung, "A Preliminary Analysis of Korean Social Stratification," in *Tradition and Change in Korean Society* (Seoul: Bum-Mun Sa, 1983), pp. 176–179.
16. Kim Young-Mo, "Sense of Social Inequality Among Koreans," *Chung-Ang Journal of Social Sciences* 1 (1987): 20.
17. Lim Hy-Sop, *Social Equality and Development* (Seoul: Choung-Um Sa, 1982); Han Sang-Jin, "A Preliminary Study on Conceptualization of Middle Stratum in Korea," *Korean Journal of Sociology* 21 (1987): 121–148; Kim Young-Mo, "Social Class Structure and Its Change in Korea," *Korean Journal of Sociology* 19 (1985): 153–169; Hong Doo-Seung, "A Preliminary Analysis of Korean Social Stratification," in *Tradition and Change in*

Korean Society (Seoul: Bum-Mun Sa, 1983), pp. 176–179; Yoo Hee-Joung, "A Study on Social Consciousness of the Middle Class," *Korean Journal of Sociology* 22 (1988): 135–154.

18. Economic Planning Board, *Social Indicators of Korea* (1988), p. 289.

19. Sim Young-Hee, *A Study of Relative Deprivation and Social Classes* (research report submitted to Ministry of Education, 1987), pp. 135–154.

20. Kim Young–Mo, "Sense of Social Inequality Among Koreans," p. 26.

21. Lee Hyo-Sun, "Attitudes Toward Labor Disputes," *Chung-Ang Journal of Social Sciences* 1 (1987): 77.

22. Kim Min-Ha, "Political Attitudes of Koreans," *Chung-Ang Journal of Social Sciences* 1 (1987): 49.

3

Labor Market Outcomes: An Overview

David L. Lindauer

An Overview of the Korean Labor Market

At the onset of the labor disturbances of the late 1980s, the majority of Korean workers acknowledged that their economic circumstances were better than five years earlier, according to survey results reported in the previous chapter. But despite such progress, the overwhelming majority of these workers expressed dissatisfaction with how their situation compared to that of other Koreans and with what they perceived was a rise in social inequality. Dissatisfaction over jobs and employers was also widespread. Before examining the roots of this dissatisfaction among Korean workers in Chapters 4, 5, and 6, this chapter documents the significant material gains Korean labor realized in the two decades leading up to the labor unrest of the 1980s. It is against this record of remarkable success that any "failures" in the Korean development model must be understood.

From Farm To Factory

One yardstick for assessing the benefits to workers of economic growth is the degree of transformation of agricultural labor into industrial employment. Kuznets highlights this transformation as one of the essential characteristics of modern economic growth.[1] The shift from farm to factory is often associated with higher labor productivity and earnings and an improvement in worker welfare.

Korean experience can be evaluated by assessing the degree and relative speed of adjustment from predominantly agrarian to mostly industrial employment. A frame of reference for evaluating the relative decline in agriculture's employment share is provided by the patterns of development approach of Chenery and Syrquin.[2] In their analysis, structural changes in an economy are related to income level and population size.

According to Chenery and Syrquin's norms, given Korea's 1986 per capita income and population, the nation had a *predicted* share of agricultural employment out of the total labor force of 33 percent.[3] The actual share was substantially lower: only 23 percent. For its income level, Korea in 1986 greatly exceeded the degree of employment transformation out of agriculture expected in an industrializing economy.

But this result alone does not mean that Korea has been more successful than other countries in achieving the structural transformation of its workforce. Going back twenty-five years to 1966, Korea's actual share of agricultural employment out of the total labor force, 55 percent, was already well below 70 percent, the value predicted by Chenery and Syrquin's international database.[4] Given Korea's rising income and population levels between 1966 and 1986, a decline of 37 percent in agricultural employment's share of the labor force is predicted. The observed decline was slightly less: 32 percent.

Korea underwent a major transformation in employment, but the rate of change is consistent with what would be expected given the realized changes in per capita income. What remains remarkable is how quickly per capita income increased and how the transformation of employment from farm to factory, with all its attendant social dislocations, could keep pace. To appreciate the speed of Korea's transformation, consider Japan's experience. Japan, a nation with a similar factor endowment to Korea, required forty-five years, from 1920 to 1965, to achieve a comparable decline in agriculture's share of total employment—from approximately 55 percent to 23 percent. Even after subtracting ten to fifteen years to account for the Pacific War and the reconstruction period that followed, Japan's structural transformation out of agricultural employment still took 50 percent longer than did Korea's.[5]

The rate of structural change in employment at best is a proxy for the benefits accruing to labor from economic growth. Rural incomes may prove competitive with those received in industrial pursuits, especially when government policies promote the agricultural sector (an issue addressed in Chapter 7). Alternatively, labor may gain little if the transformation of employment from agriculture to industry generates substantial urban unemployment or underemployment as a replacement for previously rural surplus labor.

There is considerable evidence that the transformation of Korean jobs from farm to factory generated substantial employment and minimal open unemployment. Going back to the mid-1960s, the years that ushered in

Korea's economic takeoff, the rates of open unemployment among nonfarm households were well into the teens: 14.4 percent in 1964 and 13.5 percent in 1965. The last year of double-digit rates was 1967, and they have not been recorded since. On a decade-by-decade basis, unemployment among nonfarm households has fallen. From 1964 to 1969 the rate averaged 11.4 percent, in the 1970s, it was 6.5 percent, and in the 1980s, 5.0 percent.[6] In 1988 the rate fell to a historic low of 3.0 percent. The degree of cyclical variation in unemployment has also been minor. The simple correlation coefficient between the annual rate of unemployment among nonfarm households and the gross national product (GNP) growth rate, 1964 to 1989, is only − 0.12 percent.[7]

Data on Employment and Earnings

The broad brushstrokes of Korea's labor market experience support a positive image of the benefits to workers resulting from rapid economic growth. But a fuller assessment of improvements in the material progress workers experienced requires information, extending over time, on employment, wages, and other working conditions. Available data are a constraint on the analysis and require identification of separate segments of the labor market for further study. A brief review of data sources lends an important perspective on much of the analysis to follow.

By international standards, data on the Korean economy are abundant and accurate. In the labor market area, this is true for employment series; earnings data are more limited. Earnings information can be obtained from the Ministry of Labor's Monthly Wage Survey (MWS) and Occupational Wage Survey (OWS), and from the Economic Planning Board's Survey of Mining and Manufacturing, all of which have been compiled for many years and employ sampling frames based on establishments, not households.[8] Drawing from a population of registered companies, each of these surveys fails to capture a significant percentage of workers who fall in one of the following three categories: the self-employed and family workers, public employees of government and state enterprises, and workers in small establishments (usually fewer than ten workers). A comparison of employment and earnings data reveals that the extent of missing wage data is nontrivial.

The most comprehensive source of Korean employment data is the annual Economically Active Population Survey (EAPS), but earnings data are not available from this source. The MWS and OWS provide employment and earnings data, but only for firms employing ten or more workers. The amount of employment, by economic sector, projected to correspond to the earnings data of the OWS is presented in Table 3-1 (column 2).

Table 3-1. Employment by Economic Sector, 1985

Industry	(thousands of workers)		
	(1) EAPS	(2) OWS	(3) Other
1. Total employment	14,935	3,419	—
2. Agriculture[a]	3,722	N.A.	—
3. Mining	154	72	91[e]
4. Manufacturing	3,500	2,163	2,438[e]
5. Construction	908	129	860
6. Social overhead capital and other services	6,651	1,055	—
A. Commerce[b]	—	151	1,718 (1982)[g]
B. Utilities	—	27	—
C. Transport[c]	—	369	529[f,g]
D. Finance[d]	—	228	—
E. Personal services	—	279	—
F. Public sector	—	—	671[g]

Notes: EAPS: Economically Active Population Survey; all workers.
OWS: Occupational Wage Survey, establishments of ten or more workers.
[a] Includes forestry, fishing, and hunting.
[b] Includes wholesale and retail trade, as well as hotels and restaurants.
[c] Includes storage and communications.
[d] Includes financing, insurance, real estate, and business services.
[e] From Economic Planning Board, Report on Mining and Manufacturing Survey (1985).
[f] Transport only.
[g] Reported in Economic Planning Board, Korea: Statistical Yearbook.

(Employment data from the OWS and MWS are almost identical, differing marginally due to differences in each survey's reference period.) A comparison of the EAPS and OWS employment data reveals the limited coverage of Korean earnings series. In 1985, chosen as a representative year, OWS earnings data account for fewer than one in four Korean workers. Restricting the comparison to nonagricultural employment, the ratio is slightly less than one in three. Nonetheless, it is from this limited sample that all the frequently cited basic statistics on real wage growth in Korea are derived.[9]

Out of 11 million nonagricultural workers in 1985, approximately 8 million are missing corresponding earnings data. According to a comparison with the EAPS, 18 percent of these workers are employed in mining and manufacturing, 10 percent in construction, and 72 percent in the service sector, broadly defined. The lack of coverage by the OWS of the service sector is reinforced by employment data from the Census of Wholesale and Retail Trade (Table 3-1, column 3, line 6A). The census employs no company size cutoff and reports twelve times the number of workers in similar trades as indicated by the OWS.

A second characteristic of workers for whom earnings data is missing is that they tend to work in small establishments. The low service sector employment figures from the OWS are easily explained by the preponderance of small firms involved in commercial activity. In addition, roughly one-third of the difference in total manufacturing employment reported by the OWS and the Survey of Mining and Manufacturing (Table 3-1, line 4) is accounted for by workers in firms employing five to nine. Remaining differences between the employment estimates of these two surveys can be attributed to a more inclusive definition of employment— part-time workers are more often included in the Mining and Manufacturing Survey—as well as to differences in survey reference periods and sampling methods.

Given the restricted coverage of Korean earnings data, the representativeness of the OWS for the missing earnings data must be assessed. A few straightforward adjustments can be made. Public employees, although not part of the OWS survey, are paid amounts comparable to their private sector counterparts in establishments of ten or more workers.[10] In 1985, the estimated 671,000 civil servants represented another 6 percent of total EAPS employment. Public enterprise employees, a group not covered by any specific survey, may add another 1 percent. Off-farm rural employment may account for another 10 percent of nonagricultural employment as reported by the EAPS, and this group may warrant distinct treatment relative to the urban labor force.[11] The EAPS also employs a more inclusive definition of employment, capturing part-time workers who should be netted out of the comparison. These adjustments suggest that the OWS (and MWS) earnings series may directly correspond to half of Korea's nonagricultural employees. For expositional convenience, this group will be referred to as the formal wage sector. Earnings data for a large percentage of Korea's nonagricultural workers remain missing.

Although the OWS does not survey all workers, it is likely that the results on earnings may still be representative of the missing data. If it is assumed that the labor market is essentially competitive, as it often is in Korea, and that the mix of worker skills in small versus large establishments remains in roughly the same proportions, then OWS results provide a good index of trend growth rates in average remunerations for all Korean workers. However, this is a hypothesis, not a conclusion, and further evidence is required to establish the pattern of pay for workers not explicitly covered in standard surveys. An alternative hypothesis is that formal sector employees belong to a "labor aristocracy" and that over time they have been rewarded with larger pay increases than those employed in the small-scale or informal segment of the labor market. In this situation, trends based on OWS data would overestimate economy-wide improvements in real earnings.

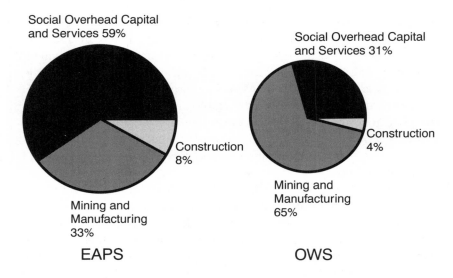

Figure 3-1. *Distribution of Employment by Economic Sector: EAPS versus OWS,*
   1985

Regardless of whether the OWS is a good predictor of the trend in
earnings for workers with missing data, competitive assumptions do not
imply that OWS earnings are a good proxy for the level of their earnings.
Interindustry dispersion of earnings exists under competitive situations,
and workers with missing data are drawn from significantly different
sectors (Figure 3-1) and, relative to their OWS counterparts, most likely
from different distributions of occupations, education levels, and so forth.
The mean wages of workers without earnings data are expected to differ
from those reported in the OWS, and, on average, they are likely to be lower.

As a strategy for dealing with the constraints of the data, the labor
market must be divided up. The formal sector permits the most analysis,
and trends in earnings and employment in manufacturing in the formal
sector are examined next. Attempts at understanding changes in labor
market outcomes for the missing half of the nonagricultural workforce
are included in Chapter 4.

Labor Market Outcomes In Manufacturing:
An International Comparison

Between 1971, one of the first years OWS data are available, and
1986, the year prior to the explosion of labor unrest, employment in

Korea's formal sector quadrupled, and the real earnings of these workers tripled. These rates of growth can be placed in some perspective by comparing them to the experience of other successful middle-income economies.

In order to make this comparison, it is necessary to restrict the comparison to formal sector employment in manufacturing. Only a small number of economies undertake surveys similar to Korea's OWS; many more employ a survey of manufacturing establishments. Although data constrain the comparison, results on manufacturing are a robust indicator for all of Korea's formal sector. Through the 1980s, manufacturing accounted for almost two-thirds of private wage employment in Korea, and although manufacturing ranks at the bottom of the interindustry earnings structure, the trend in earnings in other formal sectors, including transportation, commerce, utilities, and professional services, is well correlated with that of manufacturing. Construction, a sector that in Korea and elsewhere often exhibits more volatile wage patterns, is the only Korean industry to follow a noticeably different real earnings trajectory from manufacturing.[12]

Choosing Economies for Comparison

Placing Korean achievements in perspective requires a suitable basis for comparison. One possible approach, the one employed in discussing the transformation of agricultural employment, is to make comparisons between economies with similar per capita income. However, unlike the broad pattern of declining agricultural employment, the case cannot be as easily made for the existence of structural determinants of wage and employment outcomes within manufacturing, which levels of GNP per capita alone might capture.

As an alternative, Korean experience will be contrasted with that of other rapidly growing economies. The argument for doing so is simple. If Korean workers have done well relative to their counterparts in other successful middle-income economies, then they are likely to have outperformed workers in any broader set of economies with which their experience might be compared.

Specifically, Korea is contrasted with other large, rapidly growing, non–oil exporting middle-income economies. The period of comparison is 1965 through 1986, a distinct period in Korea's labor history. Prior to 1965, wage and employment growth were negligible or modest; after 1986, labor unrest exploded. Oil exporters are excluded from the comparison because the nature of factor rewards is significantly different under a resource-based growth strategy. The smaller city-state economies,

Table 3-2. Growth in GDP per Capita in Successful, Large, Non-Oil-Exporting, Middle-Income Countries

Country	Real Per Capita Growth Rate (%)	Real Per Capita GDP Growth Rank	GNP per Capita (US$ 1985)
Taiwan*	8.6	1	3,140
Korea	6.9	2	2,150
Brazil*	4.3	3	1,640
Thailand	4.3	4	800
Portugal*	4.0	5	1,970
Greece*	3.8	6	3,550
Yugoslavia*	3.5	7	2,070
Turkey*	2.9	8	1,080
Colombia*	2.4	9	1,320
Dominican Republic	1.9	10	790
Philippines*	1.5	11	580
Morocco	1.4	12	560
Bolivia	1.4	13	470
Guatemala	0.9	14	1,250
South Africa	0.8	15	2,010
Japan* (1950–1970)	8.6[a]	N.A.	6,930[b]

* Countries included in comparison of labor market outcomes.
[a] Real per capita GNP growth rate.
[b] GNP per capita in 1970.
Source: Kermal Dervis and Peter Petri, "The Macroeconomics of Successful Development: What Are the Lessons?" in S. Fischer, ed., *NBER Macroeconomics Annual 1987* (Cambridge, Mass.: MIT Press, 1987), Table 1, p. 214, reproduced with permission.

Hong Kong and Singapore, despite having grown rapidly due to labor-intensive export growth, are also excluded. The absence of a meaningful agricultural sector poses different constraints for the labor market and calls into question the value of making comparisons between city-states and larger economies.

Based on growth rates in real GDP per capita, Dervis and Petri provide a ranking of the fastest-growing, middle-income economies between 1965 and 1985, subject to the exclusions just noted (Table 3-2).[13] Korean labor market outcomes in manufacturing are compared with eight of the other top performers as ranked by Dervis and Petri. (These countries are denoted by an asterisk in the table and are referred to as the successful middle-income economies.) Two of the top performers, Thailand and the Dominican Republic, are excluded due to data constraints.

In addition to the successful middle-income economies highlighted in Table 3-2, Japanese experience from 1950 to 1970 is included in the comparison. The achievements of the Korean economy often are compared with those of Japan, with the view that Korea mirrors Japanese economic experience with a lag of fifteen to twenty years. In terms of

Table 3-3. Comparisons of Per Capita Income, Korea and Japan, Based on
International Prices

(Japan, 1950 = 100)		
Year	Korea	Japan
1950	55	100
1955	80	154
1960	82	226
1965	96	342
1970	140	560
1975	194	627
1980	257	740
1985	346	859

Note: Index numbers derived from each year's share of U.S. GDP per capita as reported by Summers
and Heston (1988) multiplied by U.S. GDP per capita in constant 1980 US$.
Sources: Management and Coordination Agency, *Japan Statistical Yearbook* and Economic Planning
Board, *Korea Statistical Yearbook*, various years.

national income, the similarity between the two countries is related to
rates of growth and levels of income. The growth rates of real per capita
GDP and GNP, respectively, are for Korea, 1965–1985, 6.9 percent, and
for Japan, 1950–1970, 8.6 percent. With regard to the level of national
income, appropriately lagged, Japan maintained slightly higher per capita
incomes, evident from a comparison of per capita incomes converted
according to international prices.[14] According to these data (Table 3-3),
Korea's GDP per capita in 1965 was close to Japan's in 1950, while Korea
in 1985 approximated the situation in Japan twenty years earlier. Japan's
rapid growth in the postwar period took place in a more mature economy,
but between 1950 and 1970, Japan was also a middle-income economy
experiencing rapid economic growth, supporting the comparison with
Korea.

About the Data

In selecting economies for comparison, it was important that relatively
comparable labor market data be available. For the majority of countries,
trend growth rates of earnings and employment in manufacturing could
be estimated using the results of annual (or periodic) surveys and
censuses of industrial establishments. Such surveys follow a standard
format with results reported in the United Nations's *Yearbook of Industrial
Statistics*, an annual series that extends back to the 1960s. Because of
omissions, transcription errors, and other data problems, results reported
in the U.N. *Yearbook* were considered a reference point. In most cases,
national statistical yearbooks and country-specific reports on the industrial survey were also consulted.[15]

Trend growth rates were estimated using semilogarithmic equations of the form, $ln X = a + Bt$, where X refers, respectively, to earnings and employment in manufacturing, t to calendar years, and B to the trend growth rate for each variable. The calculated growth rates are average rates representative of the available observations over the entire period. Although they do not necessarily match the actual growth rate between any two periods, they also are less dependent on the specific selection of end points. Reported growth rates refer to the weighted average of several estimated coefficients, each corresponding to a segment of the total time period during which firm size cutoffs and other survey definitions remained constant (see Appendix 3A).

Earnings refer to total real labor costs in manufacturing establishments of greater than a certain size, divided by the total number of employees (in some cases including working proprietors and family workers). The resulting series incorporates base pay, overtime, allowances, bonuses, and other pecuniary benefits and is not equivalent to a standard wage rate. Earnings were converted into a constant price series using national consumer price indices as reported in the International Monetary Fund's *International Financial Statistics*.

Initial Conditions

Prior to evaluation of relative improvements in real wages and employment in Korean manufacturing, the initial conditions of all the successful middle-income economies in the sample are compared. The employment ratio in Table 3-4 (column 3) indicates that in 1965–1966, wage-paying jobs in manufacturing accounted for only 10 to 11 percent of total national employment (including agriculture) for Korea, the Philippines, and Turkey. The potential for significant expansion of employment in manufacturing in these economies was considerable, especially when compared with Greece, Portugal, and Yugoslavia, which by the late 1960s already had more than double Korea's share of manufacturing jobs. Similar potential for real wage increases in Korea is less striking. The ratio of earnings in manufacturing to GNP per capita offers a crude proxy for cross-country comparisons of the high versus low pay status of manufacturing within an economy. Korea is at the median point in our sample, although well below the levels recorded for Turkey, the Philippines, Brazil, and Colombia.

Relatively low labor costs as well as low shares of manufacturing employment set the stage for the takeoff of Korea's manufacturing sector. Some of the other economies in the sample were in a similar position, at least regarding one of these two criteria.

Table 3-4.   Initial Conditions, 1965–1966

Country	(1) Percentage of U.S. GDP per Capita using International Prices	(2) Manufacturing Earnings/GNP per capita	(3) Manufacturing Employment/ Total Employment (%)
Brazil	16	3.07^b	16 (1976)
Colombia	19	3.04^c	24 (1975)
Greece	32	1.53^c	15 (1968)
Japan	$(17)^a$ (1950)	1.72^c (1955)	16^b (1950)
Korea	12	1.96^b	10 (1966)
Philippines	12	3.21^b	11 (1968)
Portugal	25	1.20	22 (1966)
Taiwan	15	1.21	17 (1966)
Turkey	19	3.25^c	10 (1968)
Yugoslavia	26	1.58	34 (1970)
Median	18	1.84	16

[a] Refers to 17 percent of U.S. GDP per capita in international prices in 1950. For all other countries, the base year for U.S. GDP per capita is 1965.
[b] Firms employing five or more workers; in Japan, firms employing four or more.
[c] Firms employing ten or more workers.
Sources: Robert Summers and Alan Heston, "A New Set of International Comparisons of Real Product and Price Level Estimates for 130 Countries, 1950–1985," *Review of Income and Wealth* 34, no. 1 (March 1988), pp. 1–25; United Nations, *Yearbook of Industrial Statistics*; International Monetary Fund, *International Financial Statistics*; International Labor Organization, *Yearbook of Labor Statistics*; Organization of Economic Cooperation and Development, *Economic Outlook—Historical Statistics*; Republic of China, *Statistical Yearbook;* Japan, *Statistical Yearbook*.

Trend Growth Rates

Comparison of the growth in real earnings and employment in manufacturing across the ten economies in the sample substantiates the claim that Korea has been successful in expanding well-paying jobs, at least in the formal part of the economy.[16] Employment creation in excess of the growth of labor supply would be a better gauge of performance, but reliable annual data on labor supply are not available for such a comparison.

According to the estimates of Table 3-5, Korea surpassed all the successful middle-income economies in the growth of real wages and employment. The superlative nature of Korea's experience is evident in Figure 3-2, which charts trend growth of real earnings in manufacturing against that of employment. The economies under consideration fall into four categories: (1) wage growth exceeding employment expansion (points above the ray from the origin with unitary elasticity), (2) wage growth roughly equal to employment growth (points between the lines with elasticities of 1.0 and 0.5), (3) growth in employment substantially in excess of real wage gains (points between the lines with elasticities of 0.5 to 0.0), and (4) cases of real wage decline (points below the horizontal axis).

Table 3-5. Labor Market Outcomes in Manufacturing (percentages)

| Country | Years | Annual Trend Growth Rates | |
		Earnings	Employment
Brazil	1965–1985	1.7	4.6
Colombia	1966–1986	0.6	2.9
Greece	1965–1985	5.3	2.2
Japan	1950–1970	5.4	4.6
Korea	1966–1986	7.7	8.2
Philippines	1965–1986	-1.8	3.7
Portugal	1966–1986	1.0	1.7
Taiwan	1966–1986	6.4	6.7
Turkey	1966–1986	3.4	4.9
Yugoslavia	1965–1986	1.3	4.2
Median		2.6	4.4

Source: See the discussion in the text.

Not only does Korea fall in group 2, arguably the category most consistent with the notion of expanding well-paying jobs, but Korea's annual real wage growth of 7.7 percent and employment expansion of 8.2 percent both exceed the trends reported for all the other successful countries. This outcome obviates the need to evaluate the trade-off between wage versus employment growth in judging Korean performance. By comparison,

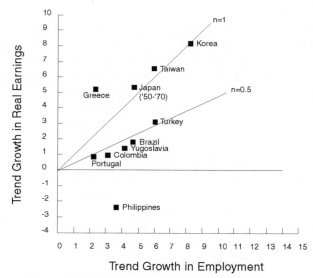

Figure 3-2. Real Earnings and Employment Growth in Manufacturing, 1965–1985 (% per annum)

Source: See the discussion in the text.

this trade-off would need to be considered in assessing Greece's experience given its relatively rapid wage but low employment growth.

How Real Is Real?

Why, then, with such a superlative record of wage and employment growth, are Korean workers apparently so dissatisfied? Before turning to more disaggregated earnings data and to nonpecuniary aspects of working life in Chapter 5, it would be useful to examine why the findings reported above, even if they had been publicized and well known, might have held little sway with the labor force of the 1980s?

First, the historically rapid transformation of employment out of agriculture implies that for much of the contemporary workforce, the perceived opportunity cost of an industrial job was no longer the toil of the farm. In 1986 the median age of a worker in manufacturing was thirty. These young people had no personal recollection of the hardships of the Korean War or of the poverty of the reconstruction period that followed. For many, urban life had been the norm since childhood. It is no wonder then that workers decreasingly appreciated the benefits accruing from the nation's structural transformation of employment opportunities.

Second, most Korean workers would likely have viewed the figures on real earnings growth with skepticism. In the 1980s, especially with housing costs skyrocketing in major urban areas, workers would have rejected the statistics on real wage trends. At almost 8 percent per annum, real earnings double in under a decade, and many working people in Korea did not believe this happened to them. At issue is less the nominal wage series than the reliability of the price deflator, the consumer price index (CPI). Criticism of reported price inflation has some basis, although the findings on Korea's impressive record of real wage growth are likely to hold up even if real trends need to be scaled back.

The arguments against the CPI are twofold: the expenditure weights are distorted, and reported inflation by expenditure category is biased downward. The primary distortion in the expenditure weights is the low share of housing costs in the commodity bundle. At 14.9 percent, the housing component is below estimates of the average propensity to consume housing services in Korea and in other countries. The old adage that one weekly paycheck a month goes to rent—that is, roughly 25 percent of a household's income is devoted to shelter—would appear to hold in many urbanized societies, Korea included.[17]

But even if Korea's CPI underestimates housing in the urban household's consumption bundle, the shortfall in the housing expenditure weight is only on the order of 5 to 10 percent. If adjusted for, this would reduce the trend in earnings because the price of housing services has increased more rapidly than the prices of all other goods, but it is unlikely to have a major impact. This is because the adjustment involves only 5 to 10 percent of the CPI (the percentage shortfall in the weight provided housing) multiplied by the marginal increase in price inflation in housing relative to other goods.

It is more difficult to ascertain the extent to which actual inflation by expenditure item is captured in official statistics since independent price surveys are rare and suffer from their own biases. The Federation of Korean Trade Unions (FKTU) has conducted cost-of-living (CLI) surveys since the 1970s. They present an annual won figure required for purchasing a market basket of goods the unions deem as minimal requirements for an urban family of four. From the published reports of the CLI survey, it is possible to employ disaggregated price information on items in the FKTU market basket of goods in constructing a price index comparable to the official CPI for the years 1981 to 1988. Over this period, the annual increase in the FKTU price series was roughly double the CPI. This result holds overall and for most expenditure categories, including food, housing, and clothing.

Is there more reason to believe the FKTU results than the official inflation numbers? As a bargaining strategy, the FKTU has an incentive to report higher price inflation, just as the government would like to report a lower amount. The CLI and CPI price series probably offer upper and lower bounds on actual price inflation.[18] Short of significant misrepresentations of price increases in the official CPI, the results of Korea's real wage performance appear robust, absolutely and relative to other successful middle-income economies.

Summary of Findings

Between 1966 and 1986, the Korean economy created about 2 million jobs in manufacturing establishments employing five workers or more. Over this twenty-year period, average earnings in these establishments, deflated by the national CPI, more than quadrupled in real terms. When added to the information on the rapid transformation out of agricultural employment and the low levels of open unemployment, the combined evidence suggests that Korean workers were partners in enjoying the prosperity generated by national economic growth.

Korea's achievements are even more impressive when viewed in relation to other successful, non-oil-exporting middle-income economies. Between 1965 and 1986, only one of the other top ten performers,

Taiwan, even came close to Korea's rate of expansion of well-paying jobs in the manufacturing sector. Even Japan's historical experience during the two decades after its post–Pacific War reconstruction fell short of Korea's rate of increase in pay and employment opportunities. But international comparisons, even if they appeared regularly in the *Dong-A Ilbo* (a popular newspaper), are not the frame of reference workers employ to evaluate their own circumstances. Although some pride might be taken in outdoing the Japanese and Taiwanese, worker expectations are not a function of cross-national performance. We must look elsewhere to understand labor's grievances and dissatisfaction.

Appendix 3A: International Comparison Data

The data used in the international comparison of labor market outcomes are generally from national establishment surveys of the manufacturing sector as reported in the United Nations' *Yearbook of Industrial Statistics*. Because of missing or incomplete data, changes in survey coverage, and apparent errors, additional national sources supplemented U.N. references. In addition, some data series were spliced together in order to maximize the quality and number of observations available. Notes on the construction of each nation's estimates follow.

Brazil
Brazilian data appear to have been frequently revised, resulting in considerable fluctuations between years and even for the same year, as reported in successive years of the U.N. *Yearbook*. The U.N. reports no results beyond 1980. The data series constructed for 1965 through 1979 were derived from the U.N. *Yearbook* employing those values that smooth out trends. U.N. results for 1970 and 1980 were excluded because they refer to census results on all establishments and are inconsistent with other years, which refer only to firms of five or more persons employed. No establishment survey appears to have been conducted for 1975. For 1981 through 1985, data were taken from the World Bank's *Brazil: A Macroeconomic Evaluation of the Cruzado Plan* (1987). In that study, Appendix Table 1.1 provides annual index numbers of manufacturing employment for 1981 through 1985. An index of average monthly wages for industrial workers is reported for 1980 through 1985 in Appendix Table 1.3. Growth rates for the entire period, 1965 through 1985, are based on the weighted average of the growth rates estimated for each of the two series.

Colombia

The data for Colombia are taken from the U.N. *Yearbook*. Annual observations were available for all variables in all years, 1966–1986, except for 1967.

Greece

U.N. data on Greece contain numerous discontinuities, so alternative sources were employed. Employment trends in manufacturing for the years 1965 through 1981 are from the Organization for Economic Cooperation and Development's *Labour Force Statistics, 1963–83* (1985); for 1982 through 1985, they are from the International Labor Organization's *Yearbook of Labor Statistics, 1987* (1987). Employment figures refer to all establishments regardless of size. Changes in reporting coverage required computing a weighted average for employment growth based on the following three intervals: 1965–1973, 1974–1980, and 1981–1985.

Japan

Data from Japan were taken from various issues of the *Statistical Yearbook of Japan*. For 1950 through 1960, the series generally refer to establishments with four or more persons employed; from 1961 through 1970, ten or more persons. From 1950 through 1960, real wages refer to firms with thirty or more regular workers and are reported as an index number. For the entire period, 1950 through 1970, weighted averages were computed for each series.

Korea

The data for Korea are as reported in the U.N. *Yearbook*.

Philippines

Firm size cutoffs on Philippine data changed on two occasions over the period under consideration. Weighted averages of all variables were constructed based on the following intervals: 1965 through 1974, firms with five or more employees; 1976 through 1982, all firms; 1983 through 1986, firms with ten or more employees. For the years 1965 through 1981, the data are from the National Census and Statistics Office of the National Economic and Development Authority, *Philippine Yearbook* (1985), Table 13.1. For 1982 through 1984, the data are from the U.N. *Yearbook*.

Portugal

The Portuguese data are taken from the U.N. *Yearbook*. However, a large discontinuity occurs in 1970, so the overall growth rates were based on the weighted averages of 1965 through 1969 and 1971 through 1986.

Taiwan

The U.N. Yearbook does not report Taiwanese data past the early 1970s, so the series were compiled from the *Statistical Yearbook of the Republic of China*. Monthly earnings are based on a labor force survey, not on the census of industrial production.

Turkey

Data are from the U.N. *Yearbook*. Changes in survey coverage required averaging growth rates of two periods: 1966 through 1982 (all public firms, plus private firms with ten or more employees) and 1983 through 1986 (all public firms, plus private firms with twenty-five or more employees).

Yugoslavia

Data are from the U.N. *Yearbook*.

NOTES

1. S. Kuznets, *Modern Economic Growth: Rate, Structure, and Spread* (New Haven: Yale University Press, 1966), chap. 3. The point is also pursued in G.S. Fields, "Industrialization and Employment in Hong Kong, Korea, Singapore, and Taiwan," in Walter Galenson, ed., *Foreign Trade and Investment: Economic Growth in the Newly Industrializing Asian Countries* (Madison: University of Wisconsin Press, 1985).

2. H. Chenery and M. Syrquin, *Patterns of Development: 1950–1970* (New York: Oxford University Press for the World Bank, 1975). For a fuller comparison of Korea relative to Chenery and Syrquin's norms, see Kim Kwang-Suk and Michael Roemer, *Growth and Structural Transformation: Studies in the Modernization of the Republic of Korea, 1945–1975* (Cambridge: Harvard University Press, 1979), chap. 6. The structural transformation of employment is not included in Kim and Roemer.

3. This value was obtained by substituting the 1986 per capita income and population of Korea into the labor in agriculture regression equation that appears in M. Syrquin and H. Chenery, *Patterns of Development, 1950 to 1983*, World Bank Discussion Paper 41 (Washington, D.C.: World Bank, 1989), Table 53.

4. The technique employed is the same as indicated in the preceding note with the exception that all values pertain to 1966 and the relevant regression equation is from Table 52 of ibid.

5. In East Asia, World War II is referred to as the Pacific War.

6. If the reported figure for the 1980s does not appear especially low by international standards, recall that the rates cited in the text refer to open unemployment rates among nonfarm households only. National unemployment rates, including farm and nonfarm households, are still lower due to the low rate of reported unemployment among members of farm households. National unemployment rates in Korea have averaged slightly below 4.0 percent since 1970 and by the end of the 1980s, at 2.6 percent, rivaled those in Japan.

7. T. Castaneda and F. K. Park, "Structural Adjustment and the Role of the Labor Market: The Case of Korea," in V. Corbo and S. M. Suh, eds., *Structural Adjustment in a Newly Industrialized Country: The Korean Experience* (Washington, D.C.: World Bank, 1992), shed light on this result by noting a significant decline in labor force participation rates rather than increases in unemployment following the economic downturn in 1980.

8. The Economic Planning Board's Family Income and Expenditure Survey, which has been conducted annually since the early 1970s, is an exception. It is household based and reports on individual earnings. This survey primarily is used to support the CPI, and published information on earnings is presented at a highly aggregated level and is not well suited for determining movements in real earnings.

9. The extensive literature on the returns to education in Korea is based on OWS or MWS data, and resulting estimates of rates of return may also suffer from sample bias.

10. Public sector compensation is discussed in Park Se-Il, "Public Sector Compensation in Korea," *Korea Development Review* 6, no. 2 (March 1984), and Park Se-Il, *Compensation in the Public Enterprises in Korea,* Policy Research Paper 86-10 (Seoul: Korea Development Institute, 1986).

11. Bai Moo-Ki, *Education, Workers' Behavior and Earnings: A Case Study of Manufacturing Workers in Korea* (Seoul: Institute of Economic Research, Seoul National University, August 1981), Table 1.

12. The time trend in interindustry earnings, 1970–1982, is presented in David Lindauer, *Labor Market Behavior in the Republic of Korea: An Analysis of Wages and Their Impact on the Economy,* World Bank Staff Working Papers 641 (Washington, D.C.: World Bank, 1984), pp. 12–18.

13. K. Dervis and P. Petri, "The Macroeconomics of Successful Development: What Are the Lessons?" in S. Fischer ed., *NBER Macroeconomics Annual 1987* (Cambridge: MIT Press, 1987), p. 214.

14. I. Kravis, A. Heston, and R. Summers, "New Insights into the Structure of the World Economy," *Review of Income and Wealth* 30 (December

1981); R. Summers and A. Heston, "Improved International Comparisons of Real Product and Its Composition: 1950–1980," *Review of Income and Wealth* 30, no. 2 (June 1984).

15. In many instances, survey and census definitions changed over the twenty-year period under consideration. Firm size cutoffs in particular varied both within and across countries. An attempt was made to eliminate spurious jumps in basic trends for individual countries by splicing together series that maintained consistent definitions. Appendix 3A describes problems encountered for individual countries, data sources, and the estimation procedures adopted.

16. Alice Amsden, *Asia's Next Giant: South Korea and Late Industrialization* (New York: Oxford University Press, 1989) arrives at a similar conclusion employing a somewhat different sample of countries. See her discussion on pp. 195–208.

17. S. Malpezzi and S. Mayo, "The Demand for Housing in Developing Countries: Empirical Estimates from Household Data," *Economic Development and Cultural Change* 35, no. 4 (July 1987), present mean rent-to-income ratios by household income for Seoul and other cities in developing nations. The values for Seoul (1979) never fall below 0.30. Estimates for other cities vary but tend to exceed 0.15. However, Korea is not alone in employing a low expenditure weight for housing in the CPI. Among the sample of successful economies employed in the comparative analysis of this chapter, expenditure weights for housing in national CPIs were as follows: Greece, 13.1 percent; Japan (1960), 9.3 percent; and Taiwan, 26.7 percent.

18. One explanation for the discrepancy between the two price series is suggested, at least indirectly, by Amsden, *Asia's Next Giant*. She notes, "Discipline has been imposed on 'market-dominating enterprises' through yearly negotiated price controls. . . . At the end of 1986, as many as 110 commodities were controlled, including flour, sugar, coffee, red pepper, electricity, gas, steel, chemicals, synthetic fibers, paper, drugs, nylon stockings, automobiles, and televisions" (p. 17). If the official CPI reflects administered prices set below actual prices, the CPI would generate a downward bias in the inflation numbers. Korean officials familiar with both price controls and the collection of price data for the CPI discount this possibility.

4

Relative Deprivation and the Distribution of Wages

Joung-Woo Lee and David L. Lindauer

An assessment of the returns to Korean labor from economic growth requires going beyond the trend in average real earnings to consideration of the distribution of economic rewards. The evaluation of any growth experience will differ according to what lies behind the average. Have the majority of participants in the economy approached the mean, or have an elite few garnered the lion's share of national prosperity?

The analysis of distributional change is fraught with difficulties. Which distributions should be examined: wages, income, or wealth? Should an emphasis be placed on functional shares, the urban-rural dichotomy, or the size distribution across households? At an even more disaggregated level, the returns to workers according to their attributes (including gender, age, and education) can be analyzed. The choice of dimension is constrained not only by the question being asked but by the availability and quality of data. Even after empirical hurdles are cleared and a quantitative picture of distributional changes emerges, the issue of fairness arises. What is a fair outcome, or, even more telling, what is perceived as fair? Furthermore, what is the opportunity cost of the observed outcome? Would a more equal or equitable outcome have required a sacrifice of some economic growth? Would a society be willing to make this sacrifice?

These difficulties confront the analysis of distribution in the Korean context. This chapter's focus is on the positive, not normative, questions. It narrowly considers whether the growth of manufacturing and other modern sector employment was characterized by gains disproportionately accruing to workers with particular attributes or if the gains were widely shared.

The Distribution of Wages

Growth in real earnings in Korea has not been concentrated among a relatively small and well-defined industrial elite. Comparable rates of wage growth have been experienced by a wide range of Korea's workers, classified according to both worker attributes and firm characteristics. Although relatively equal rates of wage growth have been achieved, the distribution of wages retains a number of pronounced pay inequalities that may have contributed to the sense of relative deprivation voiced by production workers.

The relative equality and at times progressive pattern of real growth rates in earnings are revealed by evidence on wage inequality and gross wage differentials. When changes in human capital endowments are taken into consideration, the extent to which the earnings for certain groups have fallen behind becomes more evident. Women and blue-collar workers have been particularly affected. A comparison of Korea's experience with that of other industrialized economies reveals Korea's relatively high level of earnings dispersion.

Wage Inequality

The Occupational Wage Survey (OWS) can be used to chart overall changes in the distribution of wages in Korea during the process of rapid industrialization. The survey covers firms with ten or more employees in all industries. Table 4-1 provides changes in the Gini ratio of total earnings for 1971 and 1986.[1] Various groups of workers are classified according to gender and education in order to indicate the changes in intragroup

Table 4-1. Changes in Wage Inequality (Gini Ratios), 1971–1986

	All	Male	Female	Elementary School	Middle School	High School	College
1971	.393	.342	.297	.374	.339	.304	.282
1986	.331	.278	.224	.273	.277	.266	.275

	Males by Education				Females by Education			
	Elementary School	Middle School	High School	College	Elementary School	Middle School	High School	College
1971	.321	.303	.296	.281	.238	.225	.280	.275
1986	.204	.210	.227	.266	.154	.147	.193	.294

Source: Ministry of Labor, *Occupational Wage Survey* (1971, 1986) (computer tapes).

wage inequality during the 1970s and 1980s. Changes in pay differentials between groups are considered later in the chapter.

The results show a 16 percent decline in the overall Gini ratio, from .393 to .331, during the fifteen-year period. Gini ratios also decreased among both male and female workers (with wage inequality among male workers higher than among female workers). Gini ratios, hence wage inequality, declined within all gender-specific education groups except for female college graduates.

An inverse relationship exists between the level of education and the magnitude of decline in the Gini ratios. In 1971, the higher the level of education, the lower was the Gini ratio. By 1986 wage inequality was greatest among high-education groups, perhaps reflecting increasingly varied returns to specific (as opposed to general) human capital investments. Overall, the evidence indicates that within the wage sector, decreasing wage inequality accompanied the rapid growth of Korea's economy.

What About the Small-Scale Sector?

These results on wage inequality are based on data that cover only firms employing ten or more workers. Because the OWS gives no information on the smallest firms (those with fewer than ten employees) or on the self-employed, it is extremely difficult to determine both the extent of wage inequality among workers in the small-scale sector and the wage gap between the small- and large-scale sectors. This is a serious omission because, as discussed in Chapter 3, the small-scale sector accounted for as much as half of nonagricultural employment in the 1980s.

Alternative sources are available to gain insight into wage development in the small-scale sector: the Basic Wage Survey conducted by the Bank of Korea in 1967, which was the first extensive nationwide wage survey in Korea, and the 1987 Manufacturing Wage Census of the Minimum Wage Council, conducted to determine the level of actual minimum wages in Korea. Both sources covered firms with five or more employees. Although data on firms with fewer than five employees are still lacking, a comparison of these two sources of data on manufacturing offers some insight into wage dispersion within the small-scale sector.

Gini ratios within the informal sector[2] cannot be directly computed without the raw data, but approximate values of the Gini can be obtained with the wage brackets data given in both sources by applying the Kakwani method of approximation.[3] The results are summarized in Table 4-2. Consistent with results from the OWS, wage inequality in the formal sector has decreased by a significant degree. The Gini ratio in the informal

Table 4-2. Changes in Wage Inequality in Formal and Informal Sectors, Manufacturing, 1967 and 1987

	Gini Ratios	
	1967	1987
Total	0.398	0.325
Informal sector	0.310	0.315
Formal sector	0.404	0.326

Note: Informal sector-firms with five to nine employees; formal sector-firms with ten or more employees.
Sources: Bank of Korea, *Basic Wage Survey* (1967); Minimum Wage Council, *Manufacturing Wage Census* (1987).

sector has remained essentially the same over the twenty-year period, rising from 0.310 to 0.315. Combining the two sectors, the Gini ratio has declined in total, from 0.398 to 0.325.

Further evidence of the wage gap between small and large firms is available for a continuous time series for the manufacturing sector (Table 4-3). As is true for other dimensions of the wage structure, intertemporally the wage gap has followed an inverted-**U** pattern, with the peak occurring around the early 1970s. Stated differently, when the wage gap between the informal and formal sectors is compared, there is no great difference between the early 1960s and late 1980s.[4] When this pattern is combined with the finding of declining wage inequality within each sector, the conclusion is maintained that wage inequality has decreased over the course of rapid industrialization.

Verifying this hypothesis still depends on the situation in the smallest firms (those with one to four employees) and among the self-employed, about which no information is available. Also the analysis of firms with five to nine employees covers only manufacturing. If there has been a strong trend toward inequality in the wage distribution in sectors

Table 4-3. Wage Gap by Firm Size in Manufacturing

	Firm Size						
Year	5–9	10–19	20 – 49	50–99	100–199	200 – 499	500 and over
1963	100	101	102	111	120	134	156
1966	100	104	102	114	113	140	149
1972	100	115	121	138	149	163	170
1977	100	107	111	115	117	129	148
1982	100	109	115	122	128	135	152
1987	100	103	107	114	122	130	155
1989	100	101	104	114	124	138	168

Source: Economic Planning Board, *Survey (Census) of Mining and Manufacturing* (various years).

other than manufacturing, especially services, or if the informal-formal interindustry wage gap has grown, then the hypothesis of an equalizing wage distribution across all workers would need to be modified.

Pay Differentials

There is no apparent trend toward increasing wage inequality, but what can be said about the prevailing level of inequality? Are pay differentials in Korea consistent with those observed in other industrial settings? These issues require examination of gross wage differentials and their movements over time. Examination of net wage differentials raises a different but related question: As Korea's labor force has accumulated more and more human capital, how have the returns to such investments been distributed across workers, and are differential rates of return a possible source of worker discontent?

There exists a large number of dimensions in any wage structure. Focusing on wage dispersion and human capital, earnings are related to a worker's educational attainment, experience as proxied by age, and occupational status. This is followed by an analysis of pay differentials according to gender. The section concludes with an estimation of net pay differentials and how they have changed over time, accomplished by estimating wage equations for 1971 and 1986, which simultaneously account for a broad array of worker attributes and firm characteristics.

Wage Differentials by Education

Education is one of the most important forms of human capital in which a worker can invest, and Korea has experienced an explosion in school enrollment rates at all levels over the past thirty years. It is generally argued that the movement in pay differentials by education in Korea is consistent with the forces of supply and demand in the labor market.[5]

In terms of the impact of education on wage inequality, evidence from the OWS reveals a general decline in gross pay differentials between education groups. Table 4-4 presents a time trend in earnings differentials for Korean men in manufacturing only, 1967 to 1989. Those with less than a high school education have narrowed the gap with those with more education; those with at least some college training demonstrate an inverted-U pattern, with the premium awarded college over high school education reaching a maximum in the second half of the 1970s. (The late 1970s was a time of especially strong labor demand as the economy achieved double-digit real growth rates.)

Table 4-4. Wage Differentials by Education in Manufacturing, Male Workers

Year	Elementary plus Middle School	High School	Junior College	College	Junior College plus College
1967	62.8	100	—	—	170.2
1971	71.1	100	—	—	185.8
1972	67.6	100	—	—	173.0
1973	69.5	100	—	—	183.0
1974	70.6	100	136.2	208.0	194.1
1975	70.0	100	134.6	214.8	201.2
1976	69.4	100	139.2	215.5	204.7
1977	71.1	100	139.4	211.2	197.5
1978	72.4	100	140.5	214.3	201.2
1979	76.6	100	136.7	215.1	200.3
1980	77.1	100	131.4	212.6	194.8
1981	77.7	100	128.8	206.1	189.4
1982	78.8	100	125.7	199.3	181.0
1983	82.4	100	123.1	195.1	175.9
1984	83.3	100	118.8	190.5	170.4
1985	84.5	100	117.7	189.2	168.8
1986	86.2	100	113.9	183.8	163.0
1987	89.6	100	112.0	179.8	158.5
1988	90.4	100	107.9	167.1	147.8
1989	90.9	100	108.1	161.9	144.3

Note: Relative wages of male workers with different educational backgrounds as compared to high school graduates (= 100).
Sources: Bank of Korea, *Basic Wage Survey* (1967); Ministry of Labor, *Occupational Wage Survey* (1971-1989).

The data in Table 4-4 do not appear to lend support to the notion of a labor aristocracy. One would expect such an aristocracy to be characterized by an educated workforce making disproportionately more progress in wages than the less educated segment. In the past decade, the exact opposite is revealed by the data. However, Korea's wage structure does stand out in an international comparison. The *level* of pay differentials by education, even after at least a decade of compression in the national pay structure by education, remains high.

In 1987, according to OWS data, male college graduates earned a 96 percent premium over male high school graduates—even larger than the 80 percent premium reported for 1987 for college-educated workers in manufacturing (Table 4-4), suggesting even higher pay differentials by education outside of manufacturing. Table 4-5 offers comparisons of wage differentials by education with other industrial economies. The premium going to a college over a high school education in Korea surpasses the experience in Organization for Economic Cooperation and Development (OECD) economies. The comparison is meaningful because Korea's enrollment rates in secondary and tertiary education have approached those of OECD economies for many years.[6] If the relative

Table 4-5. International Comparisons of the Wage Differential Between College and High School Graduates

	Australia (1979)	Canada (1978)	Italy (1979)	Korea (1978)	Korea (1987)	United States (1978)	Japan (1978)
Male	—	—	—	208	196	140	120
Female	—	—	—	214	250	128	127
Both	190	190	133	231	224	—	—

Note: Relative wages of college graduates as compared to high school graduates (= 100) in all industries.
Source: Richard B. Freeman, *The Changing Economic Value of Higher Education in Developed Countries: A Report to the OECD*, Discussion Paper 874 (Cambridge, Mass.: Harvard Institute for Economic Research, January 1982); Ministry of Labor, *Occupational Wage Survey* (1980, 1987).

supply of school leavers is roughly equivalent between Korea and some of the OECD economies, Korea would appear to be an outlier in terms of the premium awarded to college graduates. More disaggregated data from Japan (Table 4-6) reinforce the cross-country evidence. In 1987, college graduates in Korea received a 100 to 150 percent premium over high school graduates; their counterparts in Japan received only a 30 to 40 percent premium.

The evidence on pay differentials by education suggests the persistence rather than the emergence of wage inequalities. Stated differently, Korea's labor market has probably embodied some form of a labor aristocracy for some time. Previous attempts to explain the high returns to education in Korea are inconclusive. Park and Park, in their definitive treatment of Korea's wage structure, cite both historical and institutional forces. The historical precedent is the colonial period when educated Koreans, however few, were paid salaries equivalent to Japanese employees in the imperial state enterprises. That this legacy would persist over the course of Korea's modern economic growth is dubious. Park and Park also advance a late-industrialization hypothesis whereby the demands of advanced and imported technology put a high premium on worker knowledge and adaptability.[7] Education may serve as a signal of such skills.

Table 4-6. Comparison of Wage Differentials by Education, Japan and Korea, 1987

Education	Japan Male	Japan Female	Korea Male	Korea Female
College	127	137	196	250
Junior College	97	112	116	142
High	100	100	100	100
Middle	95	86	86	81

Sources: Ministry of Labor (Japan), *Basic Survey of Wage Structure* (1987); Ministry of Labor (Korea), *Occupational Wage Survey* (1987).

Market forces have narrowed pay differentials by education. None-theless, the dispersion in Korea's earnings structure, with pay premiums to education remaining large, may have contributed to worker discontent over the distribution of economic rewards accompanying growth.

Wage Differentials by Age

In addition to education, age, or more precisely, work experience, is a determinant of the wage structure. The steepness of the age-earnings profile has long provoked debate over the nature of labor market behavior, especially between Japan and the United States. Steeper profiles in Japan have been associated with both institutional (lifetime employment and seniority pay systems) and competitive (training and productivity effects) explanations.[8]

The age dimension of the wage structure is useful in placing the degree of pay dispersion in Korea in perspective. As is true across other dimensions of the wage structure, wage differentials by age have narrowed over the past twenty years (results not shown). Although the trend is not always strictly monotonic—there was some expansion of pay differentials by age in the mid-1970s—by 1989 the gap between young (20–24) and prime-aged (35–39) men in manufacturing had narrowed appreciably from the levels of the late 1960s.

As with pay premiums associated with education, compression in the wage structure by age has not yet compensated for what was a steep age-earnings profile to begin with. Since Japan is often associated with a strong seniority wage bias, comparison of Korea with Japan is telling. Table 4-7 contrasts the age-earnings profiles of the two countries. Comparing Korea in 1987 with Japan in 1979 or 1987 reveals Korea's even steeper profile, especially between workers aged 20-44. Whether competitive or institutional explanations can account for relatively large

Table 4-7. Wage Differentials by Age in Manufacturing—Japan and Korea, 1979 and 1987 (Men Only)

	16–17	18–19	20–24	25–29	30–34	35–39	40–44	45–49	50–54	55 and over
Japan										
1979	56	74	100	129	155	178	188	189	188	138
1987	55	76	100	127	154	179	201	212	206	164
Korea										
1979	60	77	100	146	188	213	224	229	239	228
1987	68	80	100	138	176	205	216	212	194	185

Note: Relative wages of different age groups as compared to 20-24-year-old group (= 100).
Sources: Ministry of Labor (Japan), *Basic Survey of Wage Structure* (1979, 1987); Ministry of Labor (Korea), *Occupational Wage Survey* (1979, 1987).

returns to age (experience), the evidence indicates that Korea has been characterized by a pay structure that contains much wage inequality by international standards.

Wage Differentials by Occupation

Compared to wage differentials associated with age or education, workers are even more likely to discriminate between the gains made by different occupational groups, especially between managers and production workers. Employing data from the OWS, Table 4-8 presents the time trend of the occupational earnings structure. (Appendix 4A presents the occupational classification scheme employed in the OWS. The category of professional, technical, and related workers is not included in Table 4-8 because of the high degree of heterogeneity in it.) Occupational wage differentials also followed an inverted-U pattern. The peak in the wage differential by occupation, 1976, coincides with the peak year in wage differentials for both education and age. The historically large wage premium of white-collar over blue-collar workers, *ceteris paribus*, has diminished.

Korea's occupational pay structure exhibits considerable dispersion when compared to other countries. Park and Park draw attention to this point in their examination of Korea's occupational pay structure prior to

Table 4-8. Wage Differentials by Occupation, Nonfarm Sector

Year	Managerial	Clerical	Sales	Service	Production
1971	359	204	118	90	100
1972	382	183	133	91	100
1973	406	206	151	100	100
1974	354	197	130	92	100
1975	458	215	123	104	100
1976	474	222	112	103	100
1977	439	206	131	100	100
1978	431	181	125	99	100
1979	436	176	107	97	100
1980	395	162	89	100	100
1981	367	163	96	100	100
1982	345	158	134	102	100
1983	343	155	130	101	100
1984	337	153	128	101	100
1985	340	153	136	99	100
1986	318	150	130	96	100
1987	306	144	117	94	100
1988	282	136	113	95	100
1989	258	131	102	87	100

Note: Relative wages of various occupations as compared to production workers (= 100) in all industries.
Source: Ministry of Labor, *Occupational Wage Survey* (1971–1989).

Table 4-9. Comparisons of Wage Differentials by Occupation—Korea and the United States

Country	Managerial	Clerical	Sales	Service	Production
United States (1977)	179	109	117	51	100
Korea (1976)	474	222	112	103	100
Korea (1989)	258	131	102	87	100

Note: Relative wages of various occupations as compared to production workers (= 100) in all industries.
Source: Peter Henle and Paul Ryscavage, "The Distribution of Earned Income Among Men and Women, 1958-77," *Monthly Labor Review* (April 1980), for the United States; Table 4-11 for Korea.

1980, by making reference to Germany, Japan, and Taiwan. Failing to identify a purely competitive explanation of the Korean outcome, they cite "social custom" in Korea, which values office work significantly more than production work.[9] Additional empirical evidence on the earnings gap between blue- and white-collar workers is gained through a comparison of the United States and Korea. In Table 4-9, the premium received by managers in Korea is an order of magnitude greater than in an advanced industrial economy.

Wage Differential by Gender
Unlike other dimensions of the wage structure, the male-female differential has shown little tendency toward greater pay equality. If there is a labor aristocracy in Korea, it is definitely male. However, popular sentiments concerning relative deprivation in Korea have not yet, as they have elsewhere, taken on a feminist or comparable-worth dimension. (The relationship between gender, wage inequality, and worker dissatisfaction is assessed in Chapter 8.)

Table 4-10 gives evidence of some decrease in the wage gap between male and female workers over time. But when the data are disaggregated by education groups, there is no sign of improvement in women's economic position within groups. Women always receive about 50 to 60 percent of male workers' earnings with comparable levels of education.

The relative rise in the level of women's education, along with continued sex discrimination in the labor market, yields a narrowing gap in the average wage between the sexes but not within each subcategory of educational background. This conclusion is reinforced by a more rigorous analysis of wage discrimination against women in the labor market. The wage gap between the sexes can be decomposed into two parts: one attributable to measured human capital, presumably a proxy for productivity differences, and the other due to wage discrimination.[10]

Table 4-10. Wage Differential by Gender in Manufacturing

Year	All	Elementary Plus Middle School	High School	Junior College	College	Junior College Plus College
1967	45.6	55.2	57.7	—	—	57.4
1971	43.5	53.1	62.2	—	—	69.8
1972	45.8	51.5	59.7	—	—	71.2
1973	47.8	59.3	61.0	—	—	70.7
1974	44.0	56.1	58.4	63.3	55.9	54.0
1975	42.3	54.8	57.2	64.9	56.8	53.8
1976	44.2	58.7	55.9	53.6	59.4	52.8
1977	45.5	59.1	56.6	54.4	54.5	48.9
1978	44.6	56.2	55.5	54.4	53.1	48.5
1979	43.2	53.2	53.8	53.2	53.1	46.6
1980	43.7	53.7	53.0	57.7	56.2	49.7
1981	44.8	54.5	53.3	58.4	59.2	51.7
1982	44.0	53.4	51.4	57.9	59.0	51.7
1983	44.9	52.8	52.8	55.3	64.0	52.1
1984	45.8	53.9	51.9	60.5	60.2	52.4
1985	47.0	54.6	53.4	60.7	59.1	51.4
1986	48.2	55.3	54.4	62.7	59.0	53.5
1987	50.2	55.8	56.8	58.3	53.9	49.7
1988	49.9	54.8	55.5	60.7	57.6	53.4
1989	51.2	55.7	57.5	58.6	56.6	52.7

Note: (Female wage/Male wage) multiplied by 100 for each education category.
Sources: Bank of Korea, *Basic Wage Survey* (1967); Ministry of Labor, *Occupational Wage Survey* (1971-1989).

Among the numerous decomposition methods employed for analyzing discrimination, the one developed by Blinder is adopted to analyze Korean experience.[11]

For purposes of decomposition, a regression equation of the following form is estimated,

$$ln \text{ (wages)} = B_0 + B_1 \text{ (Education)} + B_2 \text{ (Experience)} + B_3 ln \text{ (Hours worked)} + \text{error term,}$$

where wages and hours worked are measured using natural logarithms and where the B's are the estimated coefficients of the independent variables.

For the education variable, four levels of education—graduation from elementary, middle, high school, and college, respectively—are introduced as dummy variables, with high school graduation deleted to serve as a standard of comparison.[12] Labor market experience is divided into two parts—inside current firm experience (IFE) and outside current firm experience (OFE) both measured in years. All coefficients on the human capital variables were of the expected sign and degree of significance.

Summary results for the decomposition are displayed in Table 4-11a for 1971 and Table 4-11b for 1986. The gap in wages between the sexes can be decomposed into three parts: the difference in intercept (I), the difference in human capital endowments (E), and the difference in coefficients (C), that is, the difference in returns to education and experience. Wage differences attributable to differences in human capital endowments are estimated according to $C_m(X_m - X_f)$ and to differences in coefficients by $X_f(C_m - C_f)$, where C indicates the vector of coefficients and X the vector of mean values of independent variables from the above regressions. The subscripts, m and f, refer to male and female, respectively.

Among the three parts, the one related to factor endowments (E) can be associated with measured human capital and hence productivity differences between sexes. Differences attributable to the intercept and

Table 4-11. Wage Discrimination by Gender

a. 1971

	Male		Female		Endowment	Coefficient
	C_m	X_m	C_f	X_f	$C_m(X_m\text{-}X_f)$	$X_f(C_m\text{-}C_f)$
Ln (wage)		10.151		9.294		
Intercept	7.473		6.334			
Eed	-0.521	0.283	-0.801	0.542	0.013	0.001
Med	-0.322	0.283	-0.570	0.324	0.013	0.080
Ced	0.595	0.151	0.645	0.017	0.080	-0.001
IFE	0.061	0.550	0.049	3.083	3.089	0.037
OFE	0.028	12.247	0.013	5.129	0.199	0.077
Ln (hours)	0.411	5.357	0.623	5.370	-0.005	-1.138
Total					0.511	-0.793

b. 1986

	Male		Female		Endowment	Coefficient
	C_m	X_m	C_f	X_f	$C_m(X_m\text{-}X_f)$	$X_f(C_m\text{-}C_f)$
Ln (wage)		12.941		12.179		
Intercept	13.058		11.347			
Eed	-0.322	0.078	-0.333	0.119	0.013	0.001
Med	-0.179	0.251	-0.233	0.431	0.032	0.023
Ced	0.505	0.233	0.645	0.050	0.092	-0.007
IFE	0.048	5.798	0.063	3.079	0.131	-0.046
OFE	0.012	11.039	0.003	5.723	0.064	0.052
Ln (hours)	-0.107	5.412	0.134	5.434	0.002	-1.310
Total					0.334	-1.287

Note: Eed = elementary education; Med = middle school education; Ced = college and junior college education; IFE = inside firm experience; OFE = outside firm experience.
Source: Ministry of Labor, *Occupational Wage Survey* (1971, 1986) (computer tapes).

Table 4-12. Changes in Wage Discrimination by Sex

		1971		1986	
Intercept	=	1.139 }	(40.4%)	1.711 }	(55.6%)
Coefficient	=	-0.793		-1.287	
Endowment	=	0.511	(59.6%)	0.334	(43.8%)
Residual	=	0.000	(0.0%)	0.004	(0.5%)
Total	=	0.857	(100.0%)	0.762	(100.0%)

Source: Table 4-11.

coefficient terms (*I* + *C*) can be interpreted as wage discrimination in the labor market. The residual term is due to the interaction between endowments and discrimination.

The wage gap in 1971 of 0.857 in the predicted log wages of men and women can be decomposed as follows. (Summary results for the decomposition are listed in Table 4-12.) A gap of 0.511 (or 59.6 percent) is based on the difference in human capital endowments (*E*) between sexes, and 0.346 (or 40.4 percent) is attributed to wage discrimination (*I* + *C*). This implies that three-fifths of the wage gap between the sexes in 1971 was based on presumed productivity differences. The same analysis is applied to the data for 1986. For 1986, the part due to measured human capital (*E*) decreased to 0.334 (or 43.8 percent), while that due to discrimination (*I* + *C*) increased to 0.424 (or 55.6 percent).

Comparing 1971 and 1986, the wage gap computed as the ratio of average earnings between the sexes has decreased. But wage discrimination—that part of pay differentials not explained by differences in human capital—has increased in both relative and absolute terms. Women in Korea are still paid poorly when compared to men, despite the gains they have made in education and experience.[13]

Wage differentials by gender in Korea are also extremely large by international standards. Table 4-13 lists the relative hourly wages of female workers in manufacturing in all the countries reporting wage data for both sexes to the International Labor Organization. Korea is second only to Japan as far as the female-male wage gap is concerned.

Net Pay Differentials

A dominant trend in Korea's wage structure is the narrowing of most wage differentials over time. With the exception of the male-female differential, the variance in earnings by education, age, and occupation declined, although not always monotonically, between 1970 and 1989. One might conclude that on distributional grounds, Korea's workers

Table 4-13. International Comparisons of Wage Differential by Sex in Manufacturing, 1986 (percentages)

Country	Female to Male Wage	Country	Female to Male Wage
Japan	46.9	Finland	77.4
Korea	**47.8**	Sri Lanka	77.5
Czechoslovakia	67.9	Tanzania	77.8
United Kingdom	67.9	Hong Kong	77.9
Ireland*	68.7	Australia*	79.4
Switzerland	68.7	France	79.5
New Zealand	71.8	El Salvador	81.5
West Germany	72.9	Norway*	83.8
Netherlands*	74.3	Denmark*	84.9
Kenya	75.6	Sweden*	90.4
Greece	76.9	Burma	96.5

Note: Measured by hourly wages except for Kenya, Tanzania, Burma, and Czechoslovakia (monthly wages), and Hong Kong (daily wages). The year is 1986 except for Kenya (1985), Tanzania (1981), El Salvador (1985), Netherlands (1985), Switzerland (1983), and Australia (1985). Adults only for starred countries, marked with an asterisk.
Source: International Labor Organization, *Yearbook of Labour Statistics* (1987).

should have few complaints, at least in terms of a wage structure that has evolved in the direction of greater equality in relative wages.

But such a conclusion is flawed in two respects. First, although wage differentials have generally narrowed, they remain wide by international standards. Especially in a rapidly growing economy, wide wage differentials generate a significantly growing absolute wage gap, which the disadvantaged worker may come to resent regardless of the trend in relative earnings. Second, gross pay differentials fail to consider the interactive effects among the various determinants of wages. By focusing on net pay differentials, that is, on the changing contribution to earnings of specific worker attributes and firm characteristics, ceteris paribus, it is possible to identify more precisely the changing returns to specific attributes and characteristics. Of special interest is the interaction among human capital investments, occupational status, and wage rewards.

Net pay differentials are estimated (Table 4-14) using micro data from the OWS. Roughly 25,000 individual observations are available for 1971 and 1986. The wage structure in each year is estimated according to the following variables: region, sector, firm size, gender, education, age, and occupation. With the dependent variable earnings per hour (measured in natural logarithms), a comparison of the regression coefficients of the two equations permits an assessment of the net contribution of each worker attribute and firm characteristic to the wage structure, over time.[14]

Table 4-14. Changes in Net Wage Differentials, 1971–1986

Independent Variable	1971			1986		
	Coefficient	Standard Error	Probability	Coefficient	Standard Error	Probability
Intercept	4.4967	.0116	.0001	7.1685	.0088	.0001
Region						
Busan	-0.1376	.0084	.0001	-0.2149	.0079	.0001
Kyungki	-0.1499	.0092	.0001	-0.1208	.0069	.0001
Kangwon	0.0168	.0139	.2272	-0.0745	.0167	.0001
N. Choongchung	-0.1011	.0178	.0001	-0.1030	.0157	.0001
S. Choongchung	-0.2379	.0145	.0001	-0.1632	.0118	.0001
North Julla	-0.1976	.0195	.0001	-0.2501	.0136	.0001
South Julla	-0.2211	.0157	.0001	-0.0984	.0134	.0001
North Kyungsang	-0.1451	.0113	.0001	-0.1424	.0080	.0001
South Kyungsang	-0.1639	.0162	.0001	-0.0508	.0076	.0001
Jeju	-0.1156	.0390	.0030	-0.0384	.0476	.4199
Sector						
Mining	0.3337	.0139	.0001	0.3257	.0164	.0001
Elect./gas/water	0.6822	.0226	.0001	0.3693	.0244	.0001
Construction	-0.0028	.0161	.8595	0.0093	.0132	.4790
Commerce	0.2158	.0249	.0001	0.1179	.0128	.0001
Transport/ communication	0.1695	.0092	.0001	0.1154	.0083	.0001
Banking /insur.	0.5161	.0152	.0001	0.3414	.0106	.0001
Service (industry)	0.1312	.0176	.0001	0.3155	.0102	.0001
Size						
Small (10–99)	-0.2603	.0086	.0001	-0.2020	.0081	.0001
Medium (100–499)	-0.1028	.0065	.0001	-0.1150	.0049	.0001
Gender						
Female	-0.2512	.0088	.0001	-0.3695	.0065	.0001
Education						
Elem. school	-0.2698	.0090	.0001	-0.2503	.0090	.0001
Middle school	-0.1832	.0086	.0001	-0.1279	.0059	.0001
College	0.3428	.0116	.0001	0.2859	.0079	.0001
Age						
≤17	-0.3059	.0216	.0001	-0.1480	.0179	.0001
18–19	-0.1952	.0106	.0001	-0.0639	.0110	.0001
25–29	0.2348	.0102	.0001	0.1154	.0078	.0001
30–34	0.4078	.0106	.0001	0.3142	.0085	.0001
35–39	0.5362	.0113	.0001	0.4305	.0090	.0001
40–44	0.6048	.0132	.0001	0.4648	.0099	.0001
45–49	0.6853	.0162	.0001	0.4749	.0113	.0001
50–54	0.7041	.0226	.0001	0.4814	.0145	.0001
≥55	0.6396	.0423	.0001	0.4517	.0217	.0001
Occupation						
Professional-technical	0.2968	.0146	.0001	0.3111	.0101	.0001
Managerial	0.3883	.0307	.0001	0.6666	.0148	.0001
Clerical	0.1421	.0098	.0001	0.2222	.0069	.0001
Sales	-0.0591	.0393	.1327	0.0786	.0337	.0199
Service (Occ)	-0.2019	.0154	.0001	-0.2194	.0119	.0001
Degrees of freedom		26629			24140	
F value		1209.3			1707.2	
R–square		0.6269			0.7235	

Note: Dependent variable = Ln(monthly total wages/hours worked).
Source: Ministry of Labor, *Occupational Wage Survey* (1971, 1986) (computer tapes).

Each regression equation yields coefficients of the expected sign and level of significance, and the overall explanatory power of the equations is consistent with similar cross-section studies with this number of observations. Higher levels of education and employment in larger firms are associated with higher pay, while manufacturing is generally a low-wage sector, ceteris paribus. Women earn less than men, wages in Seoul almost always exceed those elsewhere, and earnings in white-collar occupations consistently surpass those of production workers.

As was true in the analysis of gross pay differentials, a narrowing of differentials is apparent along several dimensions. Compression in the wage structure continued to be evident according to both education and age/experience and, to a lesser degree, firm size. Earnings by region also narrowed, as indicated by a slight decrease in both the mean and variance in the set of coefficients on the regional dummy variables.[15] The interindustry wage structure became more compressed, with the exception of the nonfinancial services sector; the latter perhaps reflecting a compositional change within the services sector from 1971 to 1986. Also consistent with previous findings, the net pay differential by gender has increased. In other words, holding constant worker attributes and firm characteristics, female wages have fallen even further from the returns to male labor.

There is one significant difference between the trends revealed by the analysis of gross versus net pay differentials. The interoccupation wage structure expanded over time. Managerial professions have witnessed an increase in their premium over production workers from 47 percent to 95 percent, even after adjusting for education, age, firm size, and other attributes.[16] A narrowing of the occupational pay structure was revealed by the movement in gross pay differentials. This result is reversed by the analysis of net pay, suggesting that increasing human capital investments by production workers may have narrowed the gap, but returns to analogous investments have been considerably higher for the managerial group. This outcome may contribute to the explanation as to why so many blue-collar workers feel dispossessed even while their real earnings have grown.

Assessment

In absolute terms Korea's workers—male and female, educated and uneducated, in large firms and small—made tremendous material gains over the course of rapid national economic growth. The transformation of employment from rural and agricultural pursuits to urban and industrial activities stands as the clearest signal of this achievement.

In the formal sector, wage inequality declined over time, and the trend in earnings dispersion does not suggest that economic growth in Korea created a labor aristocracy. The results on improving wage equality appear robust when account is taken of the trends in the informal (but far from insignificant) sector of the economy. The data are limited, but the results on manufacturing support the findings of more casual observations. The proliferation of small-scale enterprises does not suggest a growing economic underclass of low-productivity jobs and underemployed workers. Instead, small enterprises appeared to offer remunerative and competitive employment opportunities. The narrowing of the wage gap between small and large firms suggests that workers in the informal sector were not left behind as the economy moved toward greater industrial sophistication.

Evidence on pay differentials generally reinforces the findings on the trend toward greater wage equality. Gross pay differentials in Korea, resulting from education and work experience, were narrower by the late 1980s than at any earlier time. Net earnings differentials associated with firm characteristics such as location, economic sector, and firm size also narrowed over time.

But the analysis of pay differentials also presents a conflicting point of view. First, although the trend generally was toward compression in the pay structure, the level of dispersion remained high in an international comparison. Second, net pay differentials between men and women, and between managers and production workers, widened once account was taken of human capital investments. As all of Korea's labor force accumulated increased amounts of education and work experience, the returns to these investments accrued more heavily in favor of men and white-collar occupations. Although these trends did not show up as a widening differential in wages actually received, they do point out a fundamental inequality in the pattern of economic rewards that accompanied rapid growth.

Appendix 4A: Classification of Occupations

The classification of occupations in the OWS follows the Korea Standard Occupation Classification.
0/1. Professional, technical, and related workers
01   Scientists and related technical workers
02/03 Architects, engineers, and related technical workers

04 Plane and ship (high-level) crews

05 Bioengineers and related technical workers

06/07 Medical doctors, dentists, veterinarians, and related workers

08 Statisticians, mathematicians, system analysts, and related technical workers

09 Economists

11 Accountants

13 Teachers

14 Religious workers

15 Writers and journalists

16 Sculptors, painters, photographers, and related creative artists

17 Composers and entertainers

18 Athletes and related workers

19 Workers not classified otherwise

2. Administrative and managerial workers

3. Clerical and related workers

30 Clerical supervisors

32 Stenographers, typists, and keypunchers

33 Accounting workers and related workers

34 Calculators and calculator manipulators

35 Supervisors in the transportation and communication fields

36 Traffic guides

37 Postal workers

38 Telephone operators

39 Workers not classified otherwise

4. Sales workers

42 Sales, supervisors, and purchasers

43 Technical sales workers and sales agents for manufacturing products

44 Agents in insurance, real estate, securities, and auctioneers

45 Salespersons and shop clerks

5. Service workers

50 Managers of restaurants and hotels

52 Supervisors and housekeeping and related services

53 Cooks, waiters, bartenders, and related workers

54 Housekeeping workers not classified otherwise

55   Building superintendents, cleaners, and related workers

56   Laundry workers

57   Barbers and related workers

58   Security guards

59   Service workers not classified otherwise

6. Workers in agriculture, animal husbandry, and fisheries

7/8/9. Production-related workers, drivers of transportation equipment, and menial workers

70   Production supervisors

71   Miners, quarry men, and related workers

72   Technical workers in processing of metal material

73   Technical workers in processing of wooden material and paper

74   Technical workers in processing of chemicals

75   Spinners, dyers, and related workers

76   Workers in processing of leathers

77   Workers in processing of food and beverages

79   Dressmakers, tailors, and related workers

80   Shoemakers and leather workers

81   Furniture makers and related carpenters

82   Stonecutters and related workers

83   Smiths, toolmakers, and mechanics

84   Machine installers, machine assemblers, and precision toolmakers

85   Electrical equipment installers, related electrical-electronics workers

86   Workers in broadcasting and acoustics equipment and projector operators

87   Plumbers, welders, metal plate workers, and frame-metal workers

88   Craftsmen in trinkets and jewelry

89   Glass workers and ceramic workers

90   Rubber and plastic workers

91   Paper and cardboard makers

92   Pressmen and related workers

93   Painters

94   Production related workers not classified otherwise

95   Bricklayers, carpenters, and construction-related workers

99   Menial workers not classified otherwise

NOTES

1. Earnings include regular wages, overtime pay, bonuses, and a number of readily monetized fringe benefits.

2. The terms *formal* and *informal sector* take on many definitions in the development literature. See L. Peattie, "An Idea in Good Currency and How It Grew: The Informal Sector," *World Development* 15, no. 7 (July 1987). In this context we employ the terms solely with reference to firm size.

3. See Nanak Kakwani, *Income Inequality and Poverty: Methods of Estimation and Policy Applications* (Oxford: Oxford University Press, 1981).

4. It should be noted that 1989 exhibited a large increase in pay differentials for firms over 500 workers. This outcome may have much to do with the ability of unions, after the unprecedented wave of strikes in 1987, to extract larger increases out of large firms, which may have greater ability to pay.

5. See Noel McGinn et al., *Education and Development in Korea: Studies in the Modernization of the Republic of Korea: 1945–1975* (Cambridge: Council on East Asian Studies, Harvard University, 1980), on increases in school enrollment, 1945–1975. David Lindauer, *Labor Market Behavior in the Republic of Korea: An Analysis of Wages and Their Impact on the Economy*, World Bank Staff Working Papers 641, (Washington, D.C.: World Bank, 1984), presents arguments supporting a market-based explanation of earnings differentials associated with schooling. The same conclusion is reached by Kim Dae-Il and Robert Topel, "Labor Markets and Economic Growth: Lessons from Korea's Industrialization," in Richard Freeman and Lawrence Katz, eds., *Differences and Changes in Wage Structure* (Chicago: University of Chicago Press, 1995).

6. Ideally one might want to compare stocks, not flows of education. However, school enrollment data are more readily available and highlight Korea's similarity with OECD nations:

Country	School Enrollment Rates (1987)	
	Secondary	Tertiary
Australia	98	29
Canada	104	58
Italy	75	24
Japan	96	28
Korea	88	36
United States	98	60

Note: School enrollment rates equal the percentage of age group enrolled.
Source: World Bank, *World Development Report, 1990*, Table 29.

7. Alice Amsden, *Asia's Next Giant: South Korea and Late Industrialization* (New York: Oxford University Press, 1989), also develops this theme. See also Funkoo Park and Se-Il Park, *Wage Structure in Korea*, Seoul, Korea Development Institute (1984).

8. Early accounts include Walter Galenson, "The Japanese Labor Market," in H. Patrick and H. Rosovsky, eds., *Asia's New Giant: How the Japanese Economy Works* (Washington, D.C.: Brookings Institution, 1976). More recent discussions include M. Hashimoto and J. Raisan, "Employment, Tenure, and Earnings Profiles in Japan," *American Economic Review* 75 (1985), and Jacob Mincer and Yoshio Higuchi, "Wage Structures and Labor Turnover in the United States and Japan," *Journal of the Japanese and International Economies* 2 (1988).

9. Park and Park, *Wage Structure in Korea*.

10. The issue of employment discrimination as distinct from wage discrimination is likely to operate in Korea's labor market but is not explicitly addressed here.

11. For a critique of Blinder's method, see F. L. Jones, "On Decomposing the Wage Gap: A Critical Comment on Blinder's Method," *Journal of Human Resources* (Winter 1983). See also Alan S. Blinder, "Wage Discrimination: Reduced Form and Structural Estimates," *Journal of Human Resources* (Fall 1973).

12. For the set of dummy variables, a value of one is assigned to the highest level of education attained. For example, those with at least some college are assigned to this category exclusive of all others.

13. Alice Amsden, "South Korea's Record Wage Rates: Labor in Late Industrialization," *Industrial Relations* 29, no. 1 (Winter 1990), expresses the same conclusion based on the unpublished work of Y. H. Kim, "Education and Male-Female Earnings Inequality in the Structured Labor Market: A Case Study of Korea," (Ph.D. diss., Stanford University, 1986).

14. The excluded categories in Table 4-14 are Seoul (region), manufacturing (sector), 500+ (firm size), male (sex), high school (education), 20–24 (age), and production workers (occupation).

15. The mean (S.D.) of the ten regional dummies was -0.145 (0.0732) in 1971 and -0.126 (0.068) in 1986.

16. Because the estimated equation is semilogarithmic, the coefficient must be appropriately transformed to determine the relative effect of the dummy variable. Essentially the estimated equation is of the form

$$ln\ Y = B_o + \sum_j D_j\ ln\ (1 + g_j) + \mu_j$$

where Y represents earnings and D_j the j dummy variables on the right-hand side of the equation. The estimated coefficient, c_j, of each dummy variable equals, $ln\,(1 + g_j)$, respectively, with the relative effect of each dummy variable, D_j, on Y equal to g_j. In order to extract this relative effect from the estimated coefficients the following transformation is required,

$$c_j = ln\,(1 + g_j)$$

where for small values of g, c is approximately equal to g.

5

The Quality of
Working Life

Joung-Woo Lee and David L. Lindauer

An assessment of the benefits Korean labor has received from several decades of rapid economic growth must focus on pay and employment trends. A more complete assessment of labor's experience should also take into consideration the overall quality of working life. Hours worked, job safety, labor representation, and opportunities for skill development matter to workers. Furthermore, factors responsible for rapid increases in pay and employment may not generate improvements in these other dimensions of working life. Competitive forces in Korea's labor market exerted considerable influence over wage and employment trends, while market imperfections and particular institutions may have dictated many nonpecuniary aspects of work.

Students of Japanese industrialization often emphasize improvements in the quality of working life as one of Japan's noteworthy achievements. Low turnover rates are cited as a sign of worker satisfaction; production innovations such as quality circles and zero-defect groups are popularized as humane and efficient alternatives to traditional shop floor arrangements; and lifetime employment and enterprise unions are referred to as pillars of Japan's labor relations system that supported rapid growth by encouraging harmony and group identification among blue- and white-collar workers alike.[1]

By comparison, attention to the quality of working life in Korea has been infrequent and most often is used, especially by populist reformers and radicals, to depict the dark side of labor market outcomes. Exceptionally long hours, unsafe working conditions, and rapid job turnover are cited as evidence of the price labor has paid for rapid growth in gross national product (GNP).

Working Hours

Extending at least as far back as the period under Japanese occupation, Koreans have worked long hours. In 1939, ten-hour workdays in large enterprises were commonplace, with only two rest days a month. In 1985, the average workweek at POSCO, the giant steel corporation, was fifty-six hours—forty-five regular hours plus eleven of overtime, usually mandatory, for which no premium was paid.[2] In smaller firms, working hours can be even longer. Well into the 1980s, twelve-hour shifts with short meal breaks and one day off a month were not uncommon.

For Korean firms, long working hours contributed to the low unit labor costs of Korean manufacturers.[3] From the workers' perspective, however, long hours have been one of the burdens of rapid industrialization. A 1985 survey of working conditions in Korea put it as follows:

> Of course, it is true that they earn more money by working overtime. But the physical tiredness, and no cultural and social leisure time after 12 hours of work per day makes workers mere "working machines." It is hard for them to have some kind of workers' consciousness. Their wishes are to sleep long enough, to take a day of rest, and escape from this ordeal as early as possible by making some money. A survey of women workers reveals that many of them hope to make a successful marriage thereby escaping from this miserable life.[4]

The burden of long working hours is conveyed by this quotation, but evaluation of working hours requires more than an appeal to the emotions. Historically, all industrial transitions have included a "sweat-shop" phase characterized by long hours and poor working conditions. What needs evaluation is how Korea compares with other countries. Are hours there long by international or historic standards, and if so, why has this been the case?

Empirical Trends

Various sources are available for charting the trend in average hours worked over time. The Ministry of Labor (MOL) reports information obtained from its survey of establishments, and the Economic Planning Board (EPB) obtains similar data from household surveys. Table 5-1 provides both series. EPB estimates exceed those of the MOL for all years.

Korean working hours based on household data (EPB) exceed firm-level data (MOL) for several reasons. First, establishment data exclude (while household data include) employment in firms of fewer than ten employees, and workers in small firms often face longer hours.

Table 5-1. Hours Worked per Week

Year	Nonfarm		Mining and Manufacturing	
	MOL	EPB	MOL	EPB
1970	51.6	56.1	52.9	53.6
1971	50.6	56.7	51.6	54.1
1972	50.9	57.8	51.1	56.0
1973	50.7	58.9	51.0	57.9
1974	49.7	58.0	49.6	58.4
1975	50.0	59.1	50.1	58.9
1976	50.7	59.5	52.0	59.0
1977	51.4	59.4	52.4	58.0
1978	51.3	59.3	52.5	58.4
1979	50.6	59.2	51.5	58.3
1980	51.6	58.5	52.7	56.8
1981	51.9	57.6	53.2	55.6
1982	52.1	60.3	53.3	58.6
1983	52.5	59.7	53.9	58.1
1984	52.4	58.9	53.9	57.4
1985	51.9	58.6	53.3	57.2
1986	52.5	57.0	54.2	55.3
1987	51.9	58.4	53.5	56.8
1988	51.1	58.4	52.2	56.7
1989	49.2	56.8	50.3	54.9

Sources: Ministry of Labor (MOL), *Yearbook of Labor Statistics* (various issues); Economic Planning Board (EPB), *Annual Report on Economically Active Population* (various issues).

Second, household data capture individual hours worked on second jobs and moonlighting. Third, Korea's Labor Standard Law prohibits working hours (including overtime) from exceeding sixty per week. Firms have an incentive to report hours consistent with the law; thus establishment data supplied to the MOL might contain a downward bias relative to household data.[5]

Nevertheless, in spite of their differences, both household and establishment surveys document the long workweek characteristic of Korean workers. For almost two decades, the official figures indicate an average in excess of fifty hours and reveal no sign of any secular decline, at least until 1989.

Table 5-2 compares working hours in manufacturing in 1967 and 1987, providing a more disaggregated view of how working hours have changed. Average monthly hours increased by over 10 percent, with women contributing more to this increase than men. When disaggregated by educational background, in 1987 the low-education group (elementary school and middle school graduates) worked thirty-two hours longer than in 1967; high school graduates worked fourteen hours longer than twenty years before; and college and junior college graduates worked

Table 5-2. Hours Worked per Month in Manufacturing, 1967 and 1987

	Male		Female		Both	
	1967	1987	1967	1987	1967	1987
Total	218	240	217	242	218	241
By Education						
Elementary and middle school	215	249	216	246	216	248
High school	226	242	226	237	226	240
College and Jr. college	216	214	218	213	216	214
By occupation						
Blue collar	217	251	216	247	217	249
White collar	221	215	227	209	222	214
Managerial	217	212	n.a.	208	217	211
Clerical	224	217	227	215	225	216

Sources: Bank of Korea, *Basic Wage Survey* (1967); Ministry of Labor, *Occupational Wage Survey* (1987).

two fewer hours. The same tendencies are revealed when workers are divided into blue- and white-collar occupations. During the past two decades, working hours of blue-collar workers increased by 15 percent, while those of white-collar workers decreased on average by 4 percent.

The length of the Korean workweek stands out when placed alongside the experience of other economies. Official data, as reported by the International Labor Organization (ILO) (Table 5-3), indicate that Koreans worked some of the longest hours in the world. In 1986, no other country besides Korea reported a workweek exceeding fifty hours.

Table 5-3. Comparisons of Weekly Hours Worked in Manufacturing, by Gross National Product per Capita, 1986

Country	Hours	Country	Hours
Switzerland	42.6	Ireland	41.2
United States	40.7	Spain	36.9
Norway	38.4	Singapore	48.5
Canada	38.7	Hong Kong	45.2
Sweden	38.3	Israel	38.8
Japan	41.1	Greece	39.1
Denmark	33.0	**Korea**	54.7
West Germany	40.4	Mexico	47.3
Australia	37.5	South Africa	46.7
France	38.6	Chile	44.3
Netherlands	40.3	Peru	48.5
United Kingdom	41.6	Sri Lanka	47.3
New Zealand	39.5		

Note: Nations are ranked by gross national product per capita, richest to poorest, according to World Bank estimates.
Source: ILO, *Yearbook of Labour Statistics* (1987).

Even Korea's fellow "mini-dragons," Hong Kong and Singapore, and those low and middle-income economies with per capita incomes less than Korea's, reported a shorter workweek.

A comparison can also be made between the historic experience of the now-advanced economies and Korea's current situation. To find a workweek of fifty-five hours, Korea's average in 1986 one must return to 1900 in the United States and the 1920s in Japan.[6] Measured in terms of purchasing power, Korea's per capita income in 1986 was above that of either the United States in 1900 or Japan in the 1920s, which suggests that the Korean workweek was also out of line with the historic experience of some of the now-advanced industrialized economies.

Assessment

Korea's workers in the 1980s are not likely to have known how their working hours compared to those in other countries. And even if they had such information, it is doubtful that they would have evaluated their situation based on conditions prevailing in other countries. What international comparisons provide is confirmation of the outlier status of the Korean workweek, and they encourage inquiry into explanations for this outcome.

One explanation for the length of the Korean workweek and its failure to decline before 1989 is that the long hours reflected worker preferences. In a poor economy, workers may prefer income to leisure, and a shorter workweek implicitly requires a trade-off of earnings for time. This may help to explain why Koreans worked more than citizens of more economically developed societies, but it offers less insight into why even poorer countries displayed shorter hours. A pure relative income explanation requires the assumption that Koreans, when compared to other nationalities, had a greater preference for income over leisure, a cultural hypothesis that neither lends itself to verification nor seems intuitively appealing.

A more plausible explanation for long hours can be borrowed from comparisons between the decline in European working hours since the 1940s and the flat or slightly increasing trend evident in the United States. Some observers claim a greater preference for leisure among Europeans, but others cite differential marginal tax rates and greater public provision of social services as the explanation.[7] In Europe, marginal tax rates tend to be higher and social services more heavily subsidized than in the United States. With public policy affecting the relative prices of work and leisure, even with the same preferences, Europeans, facing relative prices more favorable to leisure, would be expected to work fewer hours than their American counterparts. Owen puts it well:

> The American worker, with a lower tax on his work but with the knowledge that the education of his children, his retirement income, and the medical needs of his entire family are largely dependent upon his own earnings, would be more likely to offer more labor in the market.[8]

In Korea and elsewhere in Asia, the same mechanism may be operative. A low tax burden and minimal provision of public services may contribute to the work-over-leisure outcome revealed by cross-country evidence.[9]

Relative price effects, however, are likely to go only so far in explaining historic trends in hours worked. Many labor historians place their emphasis on institutional forces, especially trade unions and social legislation.[10] Increases in productivity and, hence, incomes are necessary conditions for reductions in working time, but the experience of the United States, Japan, and most European countries suggests that strong union or government support, or both, characterizes most historical declines in hours. Whether from the ten- to the eight-hour day, or from the forty-eight to the forty-hour week, union activity or enabling social legislation contributed to hours reductions.[11]

Government's historic support for hours reduction in Europe and the United States can be linked to institutional factors, many of which are not relevant to Korean circumstances. Concern over unemployment and the need to share available work factored into passage of the post-depression Fair Labor Standards Act (1938) in the United States, which called for a forty-hour workweek. State paternalism, especially concern over the robustness of family life, appears to be part of the European motivation for legislation, which sets out standards for mandatory vacation time. Finally, on both continents, the electoral success of populist leaders contributed to labor's ability to influence legislation affecting worker interests.

The significance of a countervailing institutional force representing labor can be demonstrated empirically, by reference to the historic record, but it is also supported by the very nature of bargaining over wages versus hours. While firms can negotiate with individual workers (or groups of workers) over wages, hours determination invariably applies to all workers in a single enterprise. The nature of the production process is such that large numbers of workers must be present over the same work period. Thus, the hours bargain must be a collective rather than an individual one. It is simply not possible to negotiate a separate and different hours arrangement with each worker, since many of the workers must be at work during the same time. Since the hours decision must be a collective one, bargaining power on the worker side depends on the workers' developing some kind of collective representation mechanism. In an environment without strong support for labor, by unions or the government, employers have more power over hours negotiations, and hours reductions are less likely to be forthcoming.[12]

If union power or government support is critical for reductions in the length of the customary workweek, then it is not surprising to observe the maintenance of long hours in Korea over past decades. The historical repression of worker organizations and the alliance between government and business interests against labor minimized the chances for hours reductions because the need for collective action on the part of workers was not met. Can we then conclude that hours in Korea are *too* long?

Undoubtedly, Korean workers would gladly work fewer hours for a given income. But the interesting question is whether Korean workers would have been willing to trade some of the increase in their individual earnings for a shorter workweek. This counterfactual cannot be readily addressed in an empirical manner.[13] The differential bargaining power of employers over hours, however, suggests that worker welfare has not been maximized.

Industrial Safety

Trends

The headline, "Victims of Industrial Disaster Up Sharply—1761 Deaths Last Year," in the *Korea Times* (July 1, 1988) calls attention to the hazardous and unsafe character of working life in Korean industry, a view supported by accounts of unsafe working conditions, such as the 1988 tragedy at the Green Hill Textile Company in Anyang, where twenty-two young factory workers died in a fire in their factory dormitory. Sleeping three to a windowless room a few steps from their sewing machines, the women were trapped by locked stairway exits heaped with sweaters they had knit that day.[14] Such tragedies are not unique to Korean industry. In 1911, 146 workers, mostly women, perished in a fire at the Triangle Shirtwaist Company in New York City; a similar number died at a toy company fire in Bangkok in 1993; many other such tragic incidents can be cited.

Data available from both the Korean Ministry of Labor and the ILO permit a more aggregate assessment of the level and trend in industrial safety. The alarming *Korea Times* headline above is put in some perspective with the aid of Table 5-4. Reported industrial fatalities, an index of overall industrial health and safety, increased significantly between 1974 and 1989. But in an economy undergoing rapid industrialization, this outcome should be expected. The transformation from traditional agricultural to such high-risk activities as shipbuilding and modern construction generates higher labor incomes as well as more job-related fatalities.[15]

More telling than the absolute number of fatalities is their frequency, or more generally, the frequency of occupational injury. As Table 5-4 reveals, the number of occupational injuries per 1,000 employed persons has steadily decreased since the late 1970s. This trend is all the more significant given that the mix of industrial employment has shifted toward more dangerous activities during this time period, with construction and manufacturing jobs increasing absolutely and in relative terms.

The change in the frequency of industrial injuries can be decomposed into intra- and interindustry effects. The change (Δ) in the aggregate accident rate between two time periods, 1 and 2, is equal to:

Table 5-4. Industrial Fatalities and Occupational Injuries

Year	Fatalities (number)	Injury Rate	Hours Lost
1974	845	31.13	2.30
1975	1,006	44.46	2.29
1976	887	43.05	2.46
1977	1,174	44.60	2.72
1978	1,397	44.83	2.74
1979	1,537	36.12	2.89
1980	1,273	36.21	2.58
1981	1,295	34.12	2.72
1982	1,230	39.77	2.80
1983	1,452	39.83	2.66
1984	1,667	35.99	2.58
1985	1,718	31.55	2.68
1986	1,660	29.92	2.79
1987	1,761	26.62	2.90
1988	1,925	24.78	2.52
1989	1,724	20.06	2.19

Note: Injury rate = Number of injuries per 1,000 persons employed. Hours lost = (Total working hours lost/yearly working hours) × 1,000,000.
Sources: Ministry of Labor, *Yearbook of Labor Statistics* (various issues), and *Analysis of Occupational Injuries* (various issues).

$$\Delta(A/N) = \sum_{i=1}^{n} \{ [(N_i/N)_1 + (N_i/N)_2]/2\} \{(A_i/N_i)_2 - (A_i/N_i)_1\}$$

intraindustry

$$+ \sum_{i=1}^{n} \{ [(A_i/N_i)_1 + (A_i/N_i)_2]/2\} \{(N_i/N)_2 - (N_i/N)_1\}$$

interindustry

for $i = 1, \ldots , n$ economic sectors,

where A is the total number of accidents, A_i is the total number of accidents in industry i, N is the total number of workers, and N_i is the total number of workers in industry i.

The intraindustry effect equals the change over time in the industry-specific injury rate weighted by the average employment share of that industry. The interindustry effect is defined as the change over time in an industry's employment share weighted by the average over time in the industry-specific injury rate.

Applying this formula to Korean data on the frequency of industrial accidents between 1974 and 1989 produces the results shown in Table 5-5.[16] The incidence of occupational injuries has declined in almost all industrial classifications, services being the lone exception. Overall, the rate per 1,000 persons decreased from 31.13 to 20.06 between these years, a difference of −11.07 injuries per 1,000 employed workers. This difference can be decomposed into an intraindustry effect of −19.24 and an interindustry effect of +8.16. In other words, the total rate per 1,000 has

Table 5-5. Decomposition of Changes in Occupational Injuries, 1974 to 1989 (rates per 1,000 persons employed)

Industry	Rates per 1000			Intraindustry	Interindustry	Total
	1974	1989	1989–1974			
Mining	126.84	113.99	-12.85	-0.22	-1.37	-1.39
Manufacturing	49.99	23.26	-26.73	-11.54	4.05	-7.49
Construction	45.49	14.18	-31.31	-6.10	7.80	1.70
Utility	12.03	6.05	-5.98	-0.04	-0.00	-0.04
Transportation/ Communications	70.66	22.42	-48.24	-4.09	-0.40	-4.49
Services	0.29	10.63	10.34	2.74	-1.92	0.82
Total	31.13	20.06	-11.07	-19.24	8.16	-11.07

Source: Ministry of Labor, *Analysis of Occupational Injuries* (1974, 1989).

decreased despite changes in industry structure that would be expected to have increased occupational injuries.

The decomposition shows that two industries, manufacturing and construction, dominate the overall picture. These two industries are analyzed in more depth employing disaggregated data. The same type of decomposition was applied to 1978, the first year the disaggregated information inside both manufacturing (about sixty sectors) and construction (four sectors) is available, and 1989. The results (not reported here) show the same pattern inside these two industries: the decline in the rates within industries more than compensates for the rise in rates due to interindustry effects.

In sum, a growing industrial labor force involving an increasing percentage of jobs in high-risk activities is associated with a greater number of industrial injuries and fatalities; however, the decreasing frequency of these events is a more appropriate indicator of conditions over time.

Summary

The results on Korea suggest that working conditions have improved but remain hazardous. Whether the level of injuries and industrial fatalities is high by international standards is more difficult to determine. According to data reported by the ILO, Korea has consistently maintained one of the highest rates of industrial fatalities among industrial and newly industrializing nations.[17] However, the variance across countries in reporting methods, requirements, and accuracy is so great as to weaken any firm conclusions concerning Korea's relative standing.

The likelihood that Korea lies on the high end of the frequency of industrial injuries and fatalities among industrial economies is certainly plausible. Long working hours are expected to be correlated with increased injury rates. The relentless pressure on firms to expand output and increase profits in a highly competitive environment encouraged employers to minimize expenditures on safety (which are directly costly and raise costs indirectly by reducing the speed of assembly activities) and pollution controls. Market forces propelled both the employment and wages of Korea's workers and contributed to improvements in the safety of the workplace. But the market alone will not ensure the safety of the workplace. Market failures abound, the result of inherent risks and assignment of liability. Without meaningful representation in government or on the shop floor, labor had no voice to pursue reforms to improve the safety of the workplace.

Job Satisfaction

One of the few available data sets purporting to measure job satisfaction comes from the Social Statistical Survey, intermittently conducted by the EPB since the early 1980s. Table 5-6 presents some of the results of this survey. Many dimensions of job satisfaction were explored, including job content, wages, working hours, and labor-management relations. Survey responses are of the form "satisfied," "dissatisfied," or "neither;" listed in Table 5-6 are the percentages of workers who answered dissatisfied on each of the four job dimensions.

Among production workers, the fraction of workers dissatisfied with their wages, hours, and labor-management relations approached or exceeded 50 percent in 1988. Clearly dissatisfaction was more widespread among service and production workers than among white-collar workers, and dissatisfaction with jobs and wages increased over time for the former groups.

Another source of information on job satisfaction is a survey of workers at big business firms in five industries characterized by monopoly or oligopolistic market structures: iron and steel, electronics, automobile, machinery, and shipbuilding. The survey was conducted in 1988 by the Korea Social Research Institute, a private research group. The sample consisted of 718 blue-collar workers from nineteen firms and 229 white-collar workers from twelve firms. The questionnaire offered multiple-choice answers, ranging from "very much satisfied," "somewhat satisfied," "somewhat dissatisfied," to "very much dissatisfied." The message derived from Table 5-7 is consistent with that of Table 5-6: the relatively higher dissatisfaction on the part of blue-collar workers,

Table 5-6. Job Satisfaction of Workers by Occupation
(percentage of dissatisfied workers)

Occupation[a]	Job Content			Wages		Hours	Labor-Management Relations
	1980	1985	1988	1982	1988	1988	1988
1 and 2	5.4	4.3	5.9	35.1	29.6	23.4	19.1
3	9.4	9.8	10.8	41.6	35.7	28.8	24.2
4	17.7	19.3	21.8	42.0	41.7	42.8	28.6
5	18.9	22.3	30.0	46.2	49.8	48.7	40.2
6	18.8	21.6	27.1	48.9	54.6	48.6	47.4

[a]Occupation code: 1 = professionals and technicians, 2 = managerial, 3 = clerical, 4 = sales, 5 = services, 6 = production workers.
Source: Economic Planning Board, *Social Indicators in Korea* (1988).

Table 5-7. Job Satisfaction of Big Business Workers

	(1)		(2)		(3)		(4)	
	White	Blue	White	Blue	White	Blue	White	Blue
Wages	3.1	1.8	50.2	30.1	37.6	44.5	8.7	23.6
Hours	5.7	5.3	38.0	32.0	38.4	38.7	16.6	24.0
Environment	7.4	3.0	51.5	18.9	28.4	36.1	10.9	42.0
Promotion	1.7	3.9	34.9	14.9	38.7	28.1	24.7	55.7
Job security	11.8	5.9	55.5	39.3	21.0	30.4	9.2	24.4

Note: 1 = very much satisfied, 2 = somewhat satisfied, 3 = somewhat dissatisfied, 4 = very much dissatisfied.
Sources: Lim Young-Il, et al., "The Consciousness of Production Workers at Big Business," and Lee Young-Hee, "White Collar Workers at Big Business," both in Korea Social Research Institute, *A Study on Korean Workers* (Seoul: Baiksan Publisher, 1989), vol. 1.

especially with promotion opportunities and their work environment, the latter a proxy for the quality of labor-management relations.

The apparent high worker dissatisfaction among production workers may be one of the reasons for the extraordinarily high turnover rates of Korean workers. American workers are characterized by much higher turnover rates than their Japanese counterparts, and arguments are often presented that this difference may be the underlying basis for the widening gap in labor's skill acquisition and labor productivity growth between the two countries.[18] As Table 5-8 illustrates, Korean workers in manufacturing have separation rates of 4 to 5 percent a month, the majority of them resignations, not layoffs or dismissals. Rates for Japanese workers are lower than 2 percent a month.

Table 5-9 lists the three major reasons workers indicate for leaving their current jobs. (These results come from the 1988 survey by the Korea Social Research Institute). When asked, "Have you ever thought of leaving your job?" over three-quarters of both blue-collar and white-collar workers answered yes. The motives for leaving, more so than the sheer numbers, are revealing.

For those who had been thinking of leaving, when asked, "What would be the major reason for quitting?" the number one answer was the same for both blue- and white-collar workers: "no future prospect." Differences lie in the second and third reasons. For white-collar employees, the reasons were positive ones, such as "to seek more job experience"

Table 5-8. Job Separation Rates per Month in Manufacturing (percentages)

	1970	1975	1980	1985	1988	1989	1990
Job separation rates	6.0	4.4	5.6	4.5	4.5	3.8	3.8

Source: Korea Labor Institute, *Quarterly Labor Review 2;* no. 4 (1989) and 4, no. 1 (1991).

Table 5-9. Job-Quitting Motives of Big Business Workers

	White-Collar Motives	Percentage	Blue-Collar Motives	Percentage
1	no future	32.0	no future	23.5
2	seek more experience	20.0	bad working environment	22.6
3	begin own business	20.0	inhuman treatment	20.9

Sources: Lim et al., "Consciousness of Production Workers," and Lee, "White-Collar Workers."

or "to establish my own business," while blue-collar workers were thinking of quitting because of a "bad working environment" or the "inhuman treatment" by their employers. Because of the small sample, these responses may not be significant. However, they are consistent with the conventional view of labor's widespread dissatisfaction with the quality of working life in Korea.

Conclusions

The portrait of working life in Korea, characterized by the world's longest workweek, unsafe working conditions, and a generally dissatisfied blue-collar work force appears robust. The average workweek of Korean workers in manufacturing in the 1980s exceeded the hours reported by any other nation. Industrial accidents, including fatalities, witnessed an increase in absolute levels, although their frequency declined even as the mix of industrial activity, including rapid growth in construction and shipbuilding, became riskier. The weakness of international data on industrial safety makes cross-country comparisons especially suspect, although there is no indication that Korea's record is an enviable one. As for dissatisfied workers, in the late 1980s Korea, not such perennial favorites as Italy or the United Kingdom, was the nation repeatedly associated with one of the most demonstrable signs of worker dissatisfaction: violent strikes and labor protests.

Korea's record on nonpecuniary aspects of working life stands in sharp contrast to the results of previous chapters, which gave Korea high marks on real earnings and employment growth and the movement toward a more equal distribution of labor income. These contradictory outcomes are not a paradox. Korean labor has benefited most in those areas where competitive forces can be successfully relied on. Over the past few decades, Korea's industrial strategy generated a rapidly growing derived demand for labor, which was a necessary condition for rapid wage and employment growth. But along other dimensions of working life, competitive forces were not enough to ensure adequate, let alone superior, performance.

The determination of weekly hours and the reduction of uncertain yet catastrophic events (like job-related fatalities) require some degree of collective action. The same can be said for the creation of trade unions or other institutions of worker voice for addressing grievances. Because of underlying market failures, government intervention, not competitive forces alone, must be called on to achieve outcomes that are more desirable in terms of both worker and national welfare. With the strong alliance between government and business in Korea, government interventions required to correct market failures and to support creation of a collective voice for labor were not forthcoming. It is no surprise that Korea's record on reducing hours and improving job safety is not as enviable as its performance on wages and employment.

One of the burdens of rapid economic growth that Korean labor was forced to assume was a quality of working life that began at a low level and was slow to improve. Was the burden worth bearing? One view is that long hours, minimal attention to worker safety, and suppression of labor organizations kept unit labor costs down and economic growth up. Rising real earnings and growth in employment opportunities that were to the benefit of labor followed. An alternative view of Korea's record of poor working conditions, beyond the burden already borne by labor, is that the legacy of the poor treatment of workers has fostered a fundamentally contentious relationship between labor and management, if not between labor and government, which is not in the nation's long-run best interest. A better path for Korea might have been to offset the bargaining power of employers in order to improve the quality of working life while simultaneously promoting rapid growth, even if some growth had to be sacrificed along the way.

NOTES

1. Historical accounts of the quality of working life in Japan can be found in Hiroshi Hazama, "Historical Changes in the Life Style of Industrial Workers," in Hugh Patrick, ed., *Japanese Industrialization and Its Social Consequences* (Berkeley: University of California Press, 1976), and Kazutoshi Koshiro, "The Quality of Working Life in Japanese Factories," in Taishiro Shirai, ed., *Contemporary Industrial Relations in Japan* (Madison: University of Wisconsin Press, 1983).
2. Alice Amsden, *Asia's Next Giant: South Korea and Late Industrialization* (New York: Oxford University Press, 1989), pp. 206, 212.

3. See R. Dornbusch and Y. C. Park, "Korean Growth Policy," *Brookings Papers on Economic Activity* 2 (Washington, D.C.: Brookings, 1987), p. 398.

4. Korean Social Missionary Council, *The Living Conditions of Laborers: A Survey of Laborers' Wages and Living* (Seoul: Poolbit Publishers, 1985), p. 32.

5. The potential bias in establishment data is suggested by Bai Moo-Ki, *Education, Workers' Behavior and Earnings: A Case Study of Manufacturing Workers in Korea* (Seoul: Institute of Economic Research, Seoul National University, August 1977). Bai's study included an independent survey of manufacturing workers and found average working hours at 60.7 per week, significantly exceeding MOL data for hours worked in manufacturing in 1976 of 52.5.

6. See John D. Owen, *Working Hours* (Lexington, Mass.: D. C. Heath and Company, 1979), and Kiyoshi Yamamoto, *Wages and Working Hours in Japan* (Tokyo: Tokyo University Press, 1982) (in Japanese).

7. John D. Owen, *Reduced Working Hours: Cure for Unemployment or Economic Burden?* (Baltimore: Johns Hopkins University Press, 1989), chap. 3.

8. Ibid., p 27.

9. Amsden, *Asia's Next Giant,* Table 4.6, and Paul Kuznets, "An East Asian Model of Economic Development: Japan, Taiwan, and South Korea," *Economic Development and Cultural Change* 36, no. 3 (Supplement) (April 1988), Table 3, present cross-country evidence illustrating Korea's relatively low share of government consumption out of gross domestic product and relatively low government outlays on health, housing, social security, and welfare.

10. Benjamin Hunnicutt, *Work Without End: Abandoning Shorter Hours for the Right to Work* (Philadelphia: Temple University Press, 1988), is representative of this view (see chapters 1 and 2).

11. According to Tsujimura Kotaro, "The Effect of Reductions in Working Hours on Productivity," in Shunsaku Nishikawa, ed., *The Labor Market in Japan* (Tokyo: University of Tokyo Press, 1980), reductions in work hours in Japan in the 1970s were conditioned by government action. Hours reductions in the 1960s were not part of any public campaign but rather the result of a tight labor market and interfirm competition to attract workers. The latter occurrence, at least through the 1980s, was not evident in Korea.

12. Owen, *Reduced Working Hours*, p. 33.

13. Data on moonlighting and truly voluntary overtime are not readily available but would be useful in examining workers' revealed preferences for income over leisure.

14. Account by Susan Chira, "In Korean Factory, a Dream Is Reduced to Ashes," *New York Times,* April 6, 1988. See also Suh Joong-Suk, "The Deadend of Human Rights: The Scenes of Industrial Accidents," *Shin-dong-ah* (July 1987).

15. It is likely that not only will industrial accidents and fatalities rise during the early stages of industrialization, but the reporting of such incidents will also be positively correlated with income growth, leading to a somewhat spurious association of accidents with growth.

16. We chose 1974 as the base year because it is the earliest year for which reliable data are available. We have no ready explanation for the sharp increase in the injury rate immediately after 1974.

17. ILO, *Yearbook of Labour Statistics* (Geneva: ILO, 1987).

18. Jacob Mincer and Toshio Higuchi, "Wage Structures and Labor Turnover in the United States and Japan," *Journal of the Japanese and International Economies* 2 (1988).

6

Toward a Social Compact for South Korean Labor

Ezra F. Vogel and David L. Lindauer

The Transition to a Negotiated System

Of all the issues that threatened to disturb Korea's rapid economic growth in the late 1980s, perhaps the most pressing was labor disturbances. From 1961 until 1987, Korean laborers worked exceptionally long hours, often for modest wages, and rarely took part in work disruptions. A dramatic change occurred in 1987 when in just two months, July and August, Korean workers initiated more strikes than in the previous quarter of a century. At the time, workers were achieving rapid wage increases along with low unemployment, and yet, paradoxically, many were prepared to press demands, even at serious risk to their job security and their companies' welfare. These protests represented a fundamental challenge to Korea's system of industrial labor relations.

Accepting the inevitability of fundamental changes in labor relations in Korea has not been immediate. The economic success of the twenty years prior to 1987 is held up as evidence of the merits of strict labor control. Unrest after 1987, and the economic problems that have resulted,[1] stand as "proof" of the dangers inherent in empowering workers' organizations. The militancy of labor is ascribed primarily to exogenous forces, especially the infiltration by radical students into the workforce. Others point to government concessions as the underlying cause of militant labor activity and excessive wage demands. Some even cite propaganda efforts by the North. These views have been held by management and government officials, who find it hard to part with the enormous advantages and extraordinary success they saw in Korea's previous policies of labor control.

In our view, Korea is in the midst of a transition away from a historically repressive system of labor control that is no longer viable. To be sure, radical student activity as well as Roh Tae-Woo's June 1987 proclamation promising political reforms played critical roles in touching off Korea's labor unrest. But it is necessary to distinguish between catalysts and the underlying causes of social change. Fundamental social, economic, and political forces were at work that made it difficult, if not impossible, to maintain the old system of tight labor control backed by state force.

The issue Korea faces is not whether a new social compact between labor, management, and government will be achieved but the nature of the new compact, the length of time it will take, and the costs that will be borne in the process. An optimistic scenario paints recent labor unrest as growing pains on the way toward reconciliation. A pessimistic view is that some groups of management and labor are still on a collision course that will bring more struggles and economic dislocation before a compromise can be reached.

A Brief Comparison with Japan

No nation has made the transition to a fundamentally different pattern of labor relations quickly and easily, without some years of unrest and groping. Britain, the United States, and Japan all went through periods of turmoil accompanied by violence and bloodshed. The same is true for Korea's labor history.

To appreciate the transition process that confronts Korea's system, it is instructive to compare its current situation with Japan's between 1945 and 1955. Of all the industrialized countries, the one with labor problems most like Korea's after 1987 was perhaps Japan after 1945, when its authoritarian pattern of labor relations suddenly fell apart. In the ten years after 1945, Japanese labor relations were in almost continuous crisis. Yet by 1955 the old *zaibatsu* and authoritarian political system had been broken up, and Japan had achieved a successful social compact between labor and management, supported by government, that helped it become a great industrial power.

In many ways it was easier for Japanese managers in 1955 to achieve a labor settlement than it will be for Korean managers in the 1990s. In 1955, Japan still had a large labor surplus, and managers could more easily drive a favorable bargain that workers found difficult to refuse. By the early 1990s, Korea had a tighter labor market, and management could not as easily control the bargain. By the early 1950s, Japan had broken the back of the most militant unions by forming second unions more sympathetic to management. By the early 1990s, with labor shortages and widespread labor militancy in the heavy industrial sector, many Korean managers continued to confront militant labor unions. In Japan in 1955, wages were still much lower than in Western countries, and labor-intensive industries were still strong. In Korea in the early 1990s, labor-intensive industries were paying wages that threatened their international competitiveness, giving little leeway for providing an improved wage package and working conditions that could satisfy labor's demands.

Japanese managers by 1955 had already reached a consensus that they could not have rapid growth without the active participation of workers and their representatives. Having seen that workers feared for their jobs and therefore resisted efforts to rationalize labor use, management was prepared to invite active labor participation. Many Korean managers in 1990 still hoped they could return to the previous authoritarian system that they found so attractive and therefore had not yet achieved a consensus that they needed the active participation of labor representatives. The Korean labor movement also was highly fragmented and remained far from achieving a consensus about labor movement goals.

The essence of Japan's 1955 social compact was that industrial laborers would do everything they could in their companies to improve efficiency; in exchange, management would give workers a fair share of profits and make every effort to provide stable, long-term employment. Labor was informed about management plans for the introduction of new technology and new management programs for increasing efficiency at the company level. The same was true at the national level, where labor was to have a key role in guiding the Japan Productivity Center. Established in 1955 as an independent agency with support from business groups, organized labor, and the government, its purpose was to monitor productivity trends and make recommendations for improving workplace productivity.

Wage negotiations were to be conducted in all companies simultaneously each year to synchronize wage increases so as to avoid spiraling wage-price inflation. Management, working through Nikkeiren (the Japanese Employers' Federation), would discuss broad issues with the national unions (the largest then being Sohyo and Domei), but wage settlements were to be made by the individual company. A basic formula for wage improvements was reached based on factors including size, market share, productivity increase, profitability, and international competitiveness, with firms in a sector ranked by size of the permitted wage increase. Unions also were allowed a political voice and supported the

Communist party, the Socialist party, or, after 1959, the Democratic Socialist party.

Korea need not adopt the Japanese model. The key point is that Japan faced labor problems between 1945 and 1955 that at the time looked as contentious as did those from 1987 through 1990 in Korea. Japan achieved a new social compact that supported continued economic progress. Korea has the potential for achieving a similar result.

The Korean Labor Relations System, 1961–1987

Until 1961, Korea's labor union movement was more of a political movement addressing national issues than a trade union movement representing the economic interest of workers.[2] During the Japanese occupation (1905–1945), the key political issue was national independence, but the fledgling labor movement that developed after 1919 was virtually snuffed out in 1931 after the Manchurian invasion, when the Japanese military tightened its control. After World War II, with Korea divided by the occupation forces of the Soviets and the Americans, the labor movement in the South, like other movements, was split between the procommunists, *Chun Pyong* (General Council of Korean Trade Unions), and the anticommunists, *Daehan Nochong* (Federation of Korean Trade Unions). *Chun Pyong* was stamped out in 1949; nonetheless, the labor movement remained primarily political in orientation and split again as popular attitudes against President Syngman Rhee intensified in 1959 and 1960.

After General Park Chung-Hee became president in 1961, he dissolved all existing political organizations, including trade unions, and formed a new national trade union, Hankook Nochong also translated as the Federation of Korean Trade Unions, (FKTU), which became heir to the earlier anticommunist unions. President Park (1961–1979) and his successor, President Chun Doo Hwan (1980–1987), like Syngman Rhee, remained preoccupied with national security issues and used the threat from the North to justify strict surveillance of and restraint on labor union activity. Government specialists on labor were more concerned with surveillance and with limiting potential sources of political opposition than with establishing a framework for labor-management negotiations.

President Park remained preoccupied with security and political concerns, but he and his advisers began to prepare for economic growth as soon as they took office. Economic growth was an urgent necessity not only to gain support from the public for a regime that had come to

power through a coup but also to provide an industrial base to resist North Korea. Leaders were convinced that South Korea did not have the luxury to allow a democratic labor movement, and in the 1960s, as Park looked abroad for foreign capital, he was determined to assure investors that they could count on labor peace. Starting in 1971, strikes were prohibited, and unions, which in the mid-1960s had been given some room to maneuver, fell under strict government supervision.[3]

By the 1970s, FKTU was tightly controlled by the government and staffed at the highest levels partly by government bureaucrats. As industrial growth exploded and the number of industrial workers grew from 780,000 in 1962 to 4,807,000 in 1980, new members were recruited. Industrial sector associations established under FKTU grew as the industries themselves grew, first in textiles, then in electronics, chemicals, and other sectors. From eleven sectors in 1961, the number expanded to twenty sectors in 1989. Higher officials of the national union generally were university graduates, different in approach and style from blue-collar workers. At the enterprise level, where union officials came into close contact with workers, some were genuinely sympathetic with the plight of the workers and tried, within the narrow limits under which they operated, to improve working conditions. The overall goal nevertheless remained political. The government's objective was to control the unions and minimize the growth of any base for political opposition.[4]

Although President Rhee in 1953 had enacted modern labor legislation at the urging of American advisers, the legislation was not well adapted to Korean society, and no one seriously endeavored to implement it.[5] Neither the provisions for maintaining labor standards (for example, concerning overtime payments, the length of the workweek, or occupational safety) nor the rights of workers to organize were respected. The government retained the power to amend labor laws and to respond quickly and flexibly to labor unrest, with physical force if necessary.

During the 1970s, Korea borrowed some elements of the post-1955 Japanese labor relations system. The Korean Employers' Association, established in 1970, was modeled after Nikkeiren to represent management interests in providing a framework for wage decisions. Most private companies determined their annual wage increases each spring to avoid spiraling wage hikes, and the government later explicitly ruled that labor contracts were to last no longer than one year. In addition to monthly wages, as in Japan, companies paid semiannual bonuses, which together amounted to anywhere from four to six months of wages. Such bonuses were intended to encourage workers to help make the enterprise successful.

Although industry-wide federations existed, the basic power in the union organization, as in Japan, was most often at the enterprise. With enterprise unionism, management hoped that workers, concerned about their jobs in the enterprise, would be restrained in their demands. When strong unions developed with too much independence, management, especially in the *chaebol*, worked with less militant workers to form second unions, so-called sweetheart unions that were more sympathetic to management, as Japanese companies also had done in the decade before 1955. Despite some similarities with Japan's 1955 social compact, the character of Korean labor relations remained closer to that of the tight, authoritarian prewar Japanese labor system that the latter had imposed on their Korean colony than to Japan's post-1955 social compact.

It is not hard to discern why Korean management should have been so pleased with the system of labor relations. From 1961 to 1987 Korean managers enjoyed the luxury of having workers of high quality willing to work long hours at wages much lower than in developed and many developing countries, without serious labor protest. Company leaders around the world are rarely enthusiastic about having their activities constrained by worker organizations.[6] When labor difficulties arose, Korean company officials could count on government officials who, backed by laws that deprived labor of virtually any legal means of protest, could arrest or physically intimidate workers who disrupted business activities. Since Korean business had started almost de novo after the Korean War, virtually all Korean businesses through most of the 1980s were run by their original founders. Strong and determined, they were perhaps even less prepared to tolerate restraints from labor unions than the more managerial leaders who began to succeed them in the late 1980s.

Compared to Japanese firms of the same time period, which were heirs to almost a century of industrialization efforts, Korean firms started with almost no technology, no managerial experience, and no trained staff. In order to industrialize at the extraordinary pace they attempted, they had to move with daring speed, have flexibility, and correct errors. Constantly under pressure to compete in the world market with more experienced, richer foreign firms characterized by more technology and better-trained manpower, Korean managers tried to make up the gaps through greater effort, and they demanded greater effort from their workers as well.

What is remarkable is that Korean workers, under a repressive system of labor control, worked so hard and so effectively to help bring about Korea's economic miracle. They worked an average of well over an officially reported fifty hours a week even into the 1980s, far longer hours than in any other industrial country.[7] No industrial work seemed too dirty or too taxing. Westerners are impressed with how hard Japanese work, but Japanese acknowledge that Koreans, with a "hungrier spirit," worked even harder. Why were Korean industrial laborers prepared to work so hard for so many years without the benefit of meaningful union representation?

The authoritarian system of labor relations worked because it was backed by a government able and willing to use force to contain any labor unrest. In addition, social and economic factors, as well as the political power of an authoritarian regime, supported the system of labor control. The generation of Korean workers who experienced the Korean War and saw their nation overrun, their physical plant destroyed, and their friends and family killed responded to appeals for sacrifice. They could see that their country, like Japan, lacked resources, and in order to survive as a nation they had to export and maintain their power against the North.

The life experiences of many of Korea's new industrial workers in the 1960s and 1970s helped make them a compliant workforce. The majority of the new workers were recruited from the countryside where farmers remained on the margin of subsistence and were desperate to improve their family's economic livelihood. Having worked in rice paddy agriculture, they had been accustomed to hard physical exertion. As low as industrial wages were, they soon surpassed rural incomes, and young men and women from farms were ready to stream into the city and live in poor squatters' quarters and spartan company dormitories in order to find more lucrative employment. In addition, over 2 million in the South had sought refuge from North Korea between 1945 and 1953, and like refugees elsewhere, they were prepared to move where necessary and to work hard to establish roots. Meanwhile, the state was too poor to provide care for the sick and aged; only the family accepted this responsibility, and to do this the family depended on the wage earner.

Since 1950 almost all young Korean males have served two or more years in the military, where they became accustomed to high levels of discipline. By international standards, industrial work may have appeared regimented, but to the vast majority of male laborers in manufacturing who were returning servicemen, it was, if anything, less regimented than the life they knew. As for the young women who filled Korea's textile, toy, and apparel factories, and later the assembly lines of electronics manufacturers, traditional attitudes of subservience to male authority, the expectation that they would leave the labor force after a few years, and their abundant supply made them an especially docile workforce.

Even after 1987, the traditional attitude that the proper worker remained subservient and did not complain was not entirely erased.[8] Many Korean company heads behaved like patrimonial owners who, even if they employed a worker for a few months or years, expected to have broader social responsibility over the workers than a merely contractual relationship. The positive side was that some owners were concerned with the overall well-being of their workers. The negative side was that many managers were prepared to exercise tight control over workers' lives even beyond their labor services. Intellectual opponents termed the system feudalistic. But many workers had not entirely discarded the traditional attitude, which accepted this framework. For workers who were less compliant or less bound by tradition, many managers were willing to use intimidation to keep them in line. They called in strike breakers, *kusadai* or company thugs, and if such measures failed, the police and the national security apparatus could be relied on to preserve order.

Beyond social and cultural factors, the entire economic scene from 1961 to 1987 was highly volatile, with companies forming, growing at explosive rates, and some going bankrupt—all at an extraordinary speed. Firms were not stable enough for a worker to bet his career on, and firms were prepared to offer what was needed to attract experienced workers from other companies. Most workers in the 1960s and 1970s were young and single and could move quickly and easily. Throughout the 1970s and well into the 1980s, turnover rates in Korean industry often averaged 4 to 5 percent per month—that is, 50 to 60 percent of a firm's workforce might change over the course of a year![9] Workers moved from one firm to another to better themselves. Many women married and left the labor force in their twenties, and many men in their thirties left firms to start their own businesses.

The combination of an overall labor surplus and a growing economy rapidly generating employment opportunities made it relatively easy for firms to recruit new workers and workers to find new jobs. Such labor market conditions made it easier to stifle worker organizations and labor's voice because exit remained an option for the workers.[10] While labor organizers undoubtedly would have preferred to exercise a collective voice in order to improve workers' lives, the opportunities for and the willingness of workers to switch employers to improve their position reduced the pressure to push for voice alternatives.

Despite authoritarian conditions, it is remarkable how quickly Korean workers learned new skills and achieved high levels of performance. Under such a system, why were laborers so eager to acquire new skills?

In the early 1960s there was a great shortage of well-educated and experienced employees, and companies were willing to pay a premium for educated workers. But the drive for better education goes far deeper, and reflects a desire to use education not only to gain pay increments and new employment opportunities but also to improve one's basic status. In the Yi Dynasty (1392–1910), there was a deep social separation between families of those who had passed the official examinations (*yangban*) and those who had not. The belief that one improved one's status through education and examinations retained its power throughout the Japanese occupation and after the Pacific War. Both government and business relied heavily on examinations and educational attainment as a credential for higher positions. It was not easy for a blue-collar worker to rise to higher positions without educational credentials, and there was a sharp separation between those who had passed exams and those who had not.

Perhaps even more important than any limited opportunities for people already in the labor force to rise through study and examination was the lesson to families that the way for the younger generation to get ahead was through education. Educational opportunities, greatly restricted during the Japanese occupation, were much wider after the Korean War, and pressure for better education came from below. Families had fewer children so they could afford to get their children properly educated. Young women who entered the labor force saved money so their younger brothers could afford to attend a better school. Poor families used their meager savings to pay educational fees.

The quality of the workforce changed within a decade or two from one with a substantial percentage of illiterates to one with 97 percent literacy by the mid-1980s, when graduation from middle school was almost universal and high school training widespread. The new entering workforce was well educated, and the transition from long hours at study to long hours at work was the norm for Korean youth.

Workers regarded their lives as difficult, but they responded to material incentives and prepared for future opportunities without major challenges to the repressive system of labor relations. The system was effective in furthering the economic goals of owner-managers and the economic and political objectives of government leaders. But the system that severely repressed labor's voice had a broader base than workers' fear of government and management repression.

Labor Disturbances and the 1987 Turning Point

Under the authoritarian system, there were few labor disturbances. Those that did occur were mostly at the times when there was a lacuna in the control system because of political disturbances. The lacuna became most prominent in 1960, when the opposition to Syngman Rhee reached its peak, and he lost his mandate; in 1970–1971, when President Park Chung-Hee was almost voted out of office, and in 1979–1980, before and after Park's assassination when political order was weakened. Labor unrest burst out again in 1987 after opposition to Chun Doo Hwan peaked and presidential candidate Roh Tae-Woo made his proclamation promising democratic reforms.[11]

Until 1987, each time the control system had a weak spot, the government eventually responded by tightening authority in general and tightening control over labor in particular. In 1961, Park responded by getting rid of all existing unions and establishing his own national labor center, under the firm leadership of those who had strongly supported him in his military coups. In 1971, following his victory amid charges of rigging the election, he created his own constitution, the Yushin Constitution, banning future elections and restricting political and labor activities. In April 1980 Chun Doo Hwan purged those labor leaders he felt he could not rely on. All third parties (including not only student, religious, and other organizations, but even labor leaders from other federations or localities) were prohibited from interfering with any enterprise's own labor negotiations. Chun also mandated the establishment of new management-labor councils in enterprises of over one hundred employees (later fifty), which were intended, in effect, to replace labor unions. In practice the councils gave only cosmetic representation to labor and allowed control to remain firmly in the hands of management.[12] Collective bargaining was essentially eliminated.

In the 1970s, unions were usually little more than officially sponsored organizations controlled by management and backed by the government. They were under such tight surveillance, their officials often under the direct control of the Blue House, that it was virtually impossible for an established union to plan a strike. Genuine labor leadership, with solid support from workers, was almost absent. The labor disturbances that did break out were largely wildcat strikes, often sparked by some incident, such as the failure of management to pay wages, the closing of a plant, or the efforts of management to create a second union. Since strikers had not gone through the long period of cooling off and mandatory arbitration that was officially required, they were technically illegal, and management could call in the police to restore order. Many of the strikers were women who expected to retire from the workforce at an early age and had less reason to worry about possible blacklisting from future jobs.

In 1970 in the East Gate market area in Seoul, where hundreds of small-scale factories were concentrated, a young male worker, Chun Tae-Il, who had been fired several times for trying to organize workers, held a copy of the 1953 labor law in his hands and burned himself to death in front of a large gathering.[13] A protest immediately erupted. Several thousand women working for many of the small companies in the area demonstrated to shorten working hours to a six-day week and eleven-hour days, and they demanded a health check once a year.

In July 1976, when one employer, the Dongil Textile Company, part of the Kukje Group, tried to bust the union with a new sweetheart union, the female textile workers in the Kuro district of Seoul staged a sit-in hunger strike. The strike was broken by a brutal police attack. In all, 124 union members were fired, and management did not concede to any worker demands.

In August 1979 when a Korean-American owner of the YH trading company making wigs took his profits back to the United States and allowed the Korean plant to go bankrupt without compensating the workers who lost their jobs, women workers staged a several-day sit-in.

In April 1980, coal miners at the Tongwon coal mine in Sabuk discovered that a union president, chosen by what they considered an unfair election, made a secret deal with the management. Then, three thousand miners and their families occupied the town. Over 350 combat police were called in, and after three days of violent clashes, order was restored.

These spontaneous outbursts represented a wide variety of types of industries but were often in small and middle-sized plants that did not have a labor union. What they had in common was that some new turn of events had ignited long-term and deeply felt grievances. Sometimes concessions were made, but police quickly subdued the demonstrations. Working hours remained long, working conditions poor, and labor's voice at best temporary and weak.

By the 1980s public opposition toward the tight control over labor activity began to grow. A younger generation that could not remember the Korean War joined the labor force. Many of them had less fear of invasion than their elders, and some became convinced that government officials used the issue of national security to maintain their own power and personal advantages. Many believed that Korea deserved a society led by educated civilian leaders selected by a popular mandate rather than military rulers who came to power by force. Some even began to question the continued propaganda the military authorities spread about North Korea.

As the South Korean economy began to improve, many people began to doubt whether the calls to sacrifice were still necessary. In addition to people with family and friends who were beaten by police but those who saw and heard about it did not always side with the authorities. Many workers were concerned enough about their own livelihood that they opposed demonstrating students and workers, who seemed to be risking disorder and the destruction of the gains they had made at such high cost. But many became a little more tolerant and sometimes even sympathetic to those who protested against authority, especially if they did not seem to be risking chaos.

Although the government monitored labor union activity very closely, it had more difficulty controlling every nook in the society, such as the university classroom. Similarly, it had difficulty controlling all groups that came to have quasi-labor union functions, particularly the Urban Industrial Mission and the Young Christian Workers. Since over one-fourth of Koreans are Christians and those who are Christians tend to be active, Christian church groups have considerable influence. In 1960 an evangelical group loosely tied with the United Methodist church founded the Urban Industrial Mission to recruit urban workers to the church. Once formed, it came to be a partially protected haven for workers in trouble with government authorities and a source of ideological and organizational leadership. Distraught workers could meet there to share perspectives with others in similar circumstances and consider ways of seeking redress. In the 1980s when Chun Doo Hwan cracked down on labor unions, some dissident workers began to work secretly through the Urban Industrial Mission or the Catholic-sponsored Young Christian Workers to organize and prepare youth for entering factories.

As early as the late 1970s, military rulers began worrying about alienated university students' having contacts with farmers and workers. They forbade students to go to the countryside and to seek jobs in the factories. Still, many students during Chun Doo Hwan's era became *uijang*, factory workers who disguised their educational background. Some church workers who had been happy to give refuge to suffering workers felt differently when the workers became radicalized fighters, but the *uijang* and those in the church who supported them began to develop programs of their own.

The number of strikes began to increase in 1985,[14] and prominent among them was a new type of labor unrest, led by workers who had disguised their student background. An estimated 2,000 *uijang* were operating in factories, mostly in the Seoul-Inchon area of Kyongyi Province, a center of light industry. These strikes, though illegal, were no longer wildcat strikes but strikes organized by *uijang* with a political agenda against the "forces of oppression." The *uijang* provided leadership to dissatisfied workers—in a sense, providing a voice for groups that lacked an outlet not provided by *eoyong*, co-opted union officials. It is probably inaccurate to claim more of a role for the *uijang* than as catalysts that touched off volatile labor dissatisfaction; however, the government and management were quick to label the *uijang* as "impure" social elements, motivated by leftist ideologies.

In retrospect, the 265 officially recorded labor disputes in 1985 and the 276 in 1986 (up from 98 in 1983) were a mere prelude to the 3,529 that broke out in 1987. In July and August 1987 alone, there were more strikes than in the previous quarter of a century; 70 percent of all manufacturing firms with one thousand or more employees experienced a strike in the second half of 1987.

The political forces underlying the repressive system of labor changed during the 1980s and exploded in June 1987. On June 29, 1987, when Roh Tae-Woo, Chun's handpicked successor, announced an eight-point proclamation to support his election bid, the government signaled it would yield considerable political authority and grant greater leeway to dissidents. From that point, the government, concerned about the upcoming elections and about incidents that might interfere with the 1988 Seoul Olympics, suddenly refrained from clamping down on labor strife. The government allowed business and labor to deal with labor-management issues without interference.

The government's decision to withdraw from labor-management disputes precipitated the chaos that followed. Overnight, the government abandoned the prevailing system of labor control without instituting any alternative framework for resolving labor problems. Many firms were unprepared to deal with their workers, who suddenly felt empowered by government inaction, and resorted to their own strike breakers, the *kusadai*.

Once it was clear to labor that the government would take a more permissive attitude, long-suppressed grievances burst out, and the center of activity was no longer the *uijang* of the Seoul-Inchon area. Strikes began at a Pusan shoe factory of the Kukje Group, a company under severe financial strain. Workers could see that the company was not well managed and that it was in danger of closing down. When the company, straining to remain in business, put even greater pressure on the workers, the latter felt it had gone too far. The strike itself was not particularly important, but when the government did not clamp down, alienated workers at nearby Ulsan began to demonstrate.

Ulsan, on the southeast coast of Korea, was the center of the government's expansion into heavy and chemical industry beginning in the early 1970s.[15] By the 1980s an industrial belt of heavy industry, including steel, machinery, shipbuilding, automobiles, and industrial chemicals, stretched forty miles along the Ulsan coast, with hundreds of thousands of new workers recruited from all over the country. Hyundai, the *chaebol* with the greatest amount of heavy industry, was especially concentrated in this area, in what had become a company city. Each year in the late summer and the early fall, the Ulsan coast is struck by a series of typhoons. The sudden burst of labor strikes that began in late summer 1987 came to be known as the Ulsan Typhoon.

The sudden wave of labor disputes in Ulsan surprised many. In 1987 few *uijang* were thought to be employed in this part of the country. Furthermore, the workers were among the highest-paid industrial workers in Korea, and their living standards were improving rapidly, even by comparison with other Koreans. Prior to 1987 the locus of most strike activity was elsewhere. Why, then, should strikes have suddenly erupted in this area?[16]

The workers in Ulsan were sharply stratified. White-collar workers had substantially higher wages and better benefits than blue-collar workers. White-collar workers were considered management and were identified with the company. They had been recruited from universities or at least better high schools. In the way they talked to blue-collar workers—the distinctions of language—they subtly expressed disdain for those beneath them who had not passed entrance examinations. When serving in the military, many of the white-collar workers had been officers. In the Korean military, not only was discipline strict even by international military standards, but officers frequently used physical punishment. The heavy industrial belt, overwhelmingly comprising male workers, had brought a barracks style into civilian life, complete with required wearing of company uniforms, short haircuts, morning calisthenics, and separate cafeterias for blue- and white-collar workers. Worker insubordination might result in men being slapped and women being yanked by the hair. Verbal abuse was common. Many civilian workers believed the time for such treatment had passed.

By the late 1970s the new recruits into heavy industry were less rural and far better educated than previous industrial recruits; a majority had at least a junior high school education and wanted to be treated with more respect. Although the complaint was not new, perhaps no other refrain was more often repeated than, "We want to be treated like human beings." Social forces, traditionally tolerant of a system of subservient workers without voice, were being replaced by new attitudes.

In July and August 1987, blue-collar workers in Ulsan turned the tables, slapping, beating, and confining managers and executives to their offices. In one of the more dramatic cases, in Korea Heavy Industries, three thousand blue-collar workers confined two thousand white-collar workers to the inside of the headquarters building and did not allow them food or drink for forty-eight hours. When the white-collar workers were released to the grounds of the plant at the end of the forty-eight hours, they were forced to kneel en masse. Two years later, white-collar workers at the plant still felt physically intimidated by blue-collar workers. No longer could they freely use physical or even social intimidation to keep workers in line.

Since the government had strongly discouraged the formation of unions in the heavy and chemical industry, Ulsan workers had had no avenue for expressing their grievances. After 1987 they fought not only to improve their benefits but also over the right to unionize. Over the next few months, after strikes and work stoppages, workers in most of these plants had won the right to unionize. They had little confidence that an FKTU affiliate, the union confederation imposed from the top in other factories, would represent their interests. Thus, they began the wave of the new "democratic" unions,[17] unions started by workers and political activists who demanded their rights rather than unions imposed by management under government guidance.

In the ensuing months, the workers began to choose their own union leaders. Neither the labor leaders nor the workers had union experience. The rank and file did not have clearly formed opinions, and often the more vocal and radical younger workers, who demanded as much as 100 percent raises, were chosen as representatives. But before they had a chance to stabilize their position, they became suspect for selling out to management or looking out for their own personal interests. Some believed management was deliberately sowing dissension among leaders. In many of the unions, leaders were thrown out and replaced several times over the next two years.

Workers could agree on little more than that they wanted unions and vast improvement in wages, benefits, and working conditions. Although annual wage and benefit packages had been negotiated in the spring of 1987, the outbreaks during July and August forced management to raise wages a second time. Over the next two years, Ulsan heavy industrial workers received a 45 to 60 percent increase in wages, and sometimes more as management tried to buy peace and keep control.

Although the Ulsan Typhoon had a profound impact on workers and unions everywhere, in many unions where there had been a framework for dealing with worker complaints over the years, the change was less profound. In industrial sectors like textiles and basic metals, where there had been a strong FKTU union that had represented the interests of the workers, the typhoon was not strong enough to upset the established pattern of relationships. Some large companies that had fought the establishment of unions, like Samsung, weathered the storm because they had dedicated managers who tried to satisfy many of the desires of the workers while simultaneously maintaining close vigilance over any proto-union activities. Although the typhoon was felt in virtually all sizable companies, even in some heavy industrial enterprises like the Pohang steel complex where a progressive management had done a great deal to look after the interests of all employees, the typhoon was not yet strong enough to upset the basic pattern of management-worker relations. Yet some other companies, like Lucky Goldstar, which had moved to establish a union in the 1960s, were not totally immune from the typhoon's effects.

The Ulsan Typhoon also had a significant impact in sectors where intensely dissatisfied workers had previously been unable to present their demands. With the relaxation of government control over union activity, even white-collar unions became thinkable, and university graduates in various callings who were incensed at previous treatment they had received began organizing. Newspaper reporters who had resented the mass firing of reporters in the early 1970s and the tight control over their writing after that time formed unions, insisting that they be given more editorial freedom. Teachers began forming unions, demanding freedom to teach what they saw as the truth. Professionals and service staff at research institutes, including those under government direction, joined together to form unions to fight for their intellectual independence and greater benefits. To trade unionists, some of these demands hardly seemed like the arena for union activity, but given the history of political repression and the limits placed on any form of organized dissent, the use of unions for making such protests should hardly have been surprising.

What was common to all the new "democratic" unions was that these groups had not been previously unionized and they had powerful grievances previously kept in check by the threat of government repression. Dissatisfied workers and professionals who had never before participated in labor union activity had begun to talk with others who were similarly dissatisfied. Since the law was that any group of thirty who wished to form a union could do so but that only one union could represent workers' views in any particular plant, different groups of workers often began to vie with each other to form a union or to gain dominance in the union that was formed. In the midst of tensions between labor and management, leadership in these new unions gravitated to the more radical members—those most willing to make huge demands, risk job loss, and take part in militant action. Less militant workers supported them, hoping to gain from their more extreme behavior.

The new "democratic" unions considered the FKTU too conservative, too corrupt and self-centered, and too much under the control of management and the government to represent their interests. To be sure, some of the new unions found instances when their interests coincided with FKTU and they could cooperate. But by and large they viewed FKTU as too beholden to the establishment, too bureaucratic, and too set in its ways to respond to the strong demands from below. By 1987, the FKTU had little credibility as an organization that could represent the voice of labor. Even local unions under the FKTU umbrella lost confidence in the ability of FKTU headquarters to represent them effectively.

The interests of the new "democratic" unions were highly diverse, from young women who received relatively low pay in short-term work in labor-intensive small shops, to mature men who were among the highest-paid workers in large, heavy industry companies. By late 1989, the new trade unions claimed the allegiance of some 300,000 and were united in a loose council drawn together more by their common demand for industrial democracy than by specific trade union demands. The council (Chun No Hyop, National Council of Trade Union) became official in January 1990 despite heavy government opposition.

The FKTU came under great pressure to respond more forcefully to the voice of labor. At their conference in November 1988, in the direct election of the president by membership representatives, FKTU selected Park Jong-Keun. Park, known for his effective pursuit of worker interests as head of the textile union under FKTU, had been so vocal that he was pushed out of his position by the government at the beginning of Chun Doo Hwan's presidency. He was widely respected by worker representatives and by independent intellectuals specializing in Korean labor-management relations.

FKTU officials argued that in 1988 and 1989, the FKTU, pushed from below by the pressures of the new unions, became more responsive to the demands of labor and thereby began to regain credibility from rank-and-file workers. They pointed to the growth of FKTU membership in 1988 and 1989, which claimed about 1.7 million (about 1 million dues-paying members, the rest nominally affiliated) by mid-1989, while the new unions at their peak claimed only 0.3 million workers.[18] New union leaders argued that President Park Jong-Keun had been unable to bring many changes to FKTU because of the conservative industrial-sector unions that control FKTU decision making and because of the entrenched bureaucracy. In their view, the new unions would grow at the expense of FKTU.

Business leaders, alarmed by labor strife and the high wage increases they had been forced to make, began by late 1988 to urge the government to crack down on labor activity. Because unions had rarely gone through the lengthy and complicated procedure of waiting and arbitration, their strikes were technically illegal. Management argued that they were merely encouraging the government to enforce the laws and that, given a few years more grace, they could consolidate economic growth. By the end of 1988, government leaders surmised that the general public, originally sympathetic with many labor protests, had grown weary of them. A subway strike had tied up transportation in Seoul. Strikes of transport workers had wreaked havoc with the transport of goods. As a result, in January 1989 the government began enforcing the laws. They arrested strikers, called in masses of unionized workers for questioning, and jailed, according to government figures, some 200 to 300 strike leaders for "illegal activities." Strike activities were partially contained, but large masses of workers and ordinary citizens who opposed the crackdown were further alienated.

Despite the temporary lull after the 1989 crackdown, many forces were operating to bring an end to the system of repressive labor control. Traditional passive attitudes toward authority were being partially eroded, and the necessity of making sacrifices was being questioned. Public opposition to military control and demands for democratic procedures had grown. New institutions, like the "democratic" trade union movement, had acquired a base of power and could not easily be dislodged.

Furthermore, the economy was no longer the same. Industrial employment had nearly tripled during the 1970s; but between 1980 and 1987, it expanded only by 50 percent. Rising labor costs, the move toward more capital-intensive products and production methods, and the movement by Korean firms of more labor-intensive operations offshore contributed to the slowdown in the expansion of employment opportunities. As macroeconomic events brought a decline in exit options, workers turned to the establishment of voice mechanisms to achieve improvements in pay and, more generally, in their working lives.

Why Were Workers So Angry?

There remains a strange paradox. By any measure, the Korean economy for the three decades beginning in the 1960s was one of the rare success stories of world economic history, and Korean citizens, including industrial workers, have received great economic benefits, which generally have kept pace with economic progress. And yet the anger (*han*, suppressed righteous indignation) of Korean workers at their government, political leaders, business, the system, and often their own companies was profound and deep. In order to create a new social compact with labor, the roots of this anger must be understood and addressed.

Our impression, after talking with people from different circles in government, business, academe, and labor is that, despite the demand for more wages and benefits, there were four essential causes of the anger.

1. *The excessive prolongation of authoritarian controls that favored management over workers.* Workers were relatively pliant prior to the 1980s because of their fear about not finding work, their fear of invasion from the North, the cultural tradition of compliance in a paternalistic setting, and intimidation by police. The climate began to change in the 1970s as the labor market tightened and fear of invasion from the North declined. As people raised their standard of living and learned more about the outside world, they came to expect more.

Management and some government leaders, so pleased with what they enjoyed—an extraordinarily dedicated, uncomplaining, flexible, and low-cost labor force—tried to preserve the system that had begun to fall apart. The result was increased fury on the part of many laborers at a repressive system they could no longer tolerate. In a sense, the strikes were a delayed cost of the earlier repression, with roots dating back as far as the Japanese occupation.

2. *Outrage at the disrespectful treatment by superiors.* Just like Koreans, in general, who felt outraged at the lack of respect that Japanese showed them, and people from Cholla who bristled at the lack of respect that Koreans from elsewhere showed them, many workers felt outraged at the lack of respect that company officials displayed toward them.

Outrage over how workers were treated is consistent with the high levels of dissatisfaction over labor-management relations and the work environment reported for production workers in the previous chapter (see Tables 5-6 and 5-7). Such feelings are not unknown in other countries, but in Korea they seemed much more intense.

The reason seems to be a mixture of cultural attitudes and historical experiences. Educated Koreans, especially those who passed examinations, often possessed a feeling of superiority and a measure of disdain for those who had not done as well. A wide gulf separated white- and blue-collar workers. And yet those lower in the hierarchy did not fully accept status differences. They strongly believed that they were just as good as those in higher positions and that they would be doing just as well given equal connections. Uneducated recruits from the countryside in an earlier era at least partly acknowledged that they had lower status, but a new generation of workers with middle and senior high school training, many from urban backgrounds, felt that they had arrived at a higher status and expected to be treated accordingly. Workers did not fully accept the legitimacy of those in higher positions to be there, and some in higher positions believed that to get compliance from those beneath them required flaunting their status and power.

The result may be a vicious circle. When workers resent being looked down on and do not respond to flaunting of power, those in authority must flaunt it all the more to get the desired compliance. The underling then feels greater *han* even though he himself might behave the same way when he later rises to a position of prominence.

3. *An acute sense of relative deprivation.* Despite rapidly rising real wages, Korean workers perceived vast differences between their own circumstances and the consumption level of the nouveau riche. These perceptions were due to many factors. First, even if the distributions of income and wealth had remained relatively constant over the course of Korea's economic development, the absolute gap between the income levels of the working class and the business elite had grown tremendously. Second, further enlarging this absolute gap was the growing inequality in the distribution of wealth.[19] Third was the rise during the 1980s in the conspicuous consumption by newly affluent Koreans.

The upper-income brackets in Korea began a more flamboyant display of wealth in the late 1980s when the average annual income in the society was less than $3,000, lower than in some other East Asian economies when flamboyant display of wealth blossomed. In Japan, ownership in most large corporations had been separated from control even before World War II. The leaders of major Japanese companies after

World War II were salaried employees rather than owners, and the salary differentials were much lower than between Korean workers and their top company officials. By the late 1970s, when the conspicuous display of wealth had become fairly pronounced in Japan, the Japanese worker was working on average not much more than an officially reported forty hours per week, and the standard of living of the average Japanese was sufficiently high that some 90 percent identified with the middle class. Compared to Taiwan, where there were few very large companies and less concentration of wealth, Korea had large *chaebol* headed by the founding businessmen, and workers in Korea, especially in the export sector, not only worked longer hours but had lower incomes.

In the late 1980s, as pressure from the United States and other trading partners for trade liberalization began to have an impact, South Korea relaxed its import controls on luxury items, and many rich Koreans began to acquire material goods that were highly visible. Although Taiwan's display of wealth became pronounced at about the same time, average wages in Taiwan were then almost twice those in Korea.

The sense of relative deprivation was heightened because of the acute shortage of satisfactory housing for urban workers. No other Asian country suffered the destruction of housing that Korea experienced as a result of the Korean War. With the effort to channel funds for industrial investment, the construction of new housing was a low priority, and housing markets remained extremely tight. In the 1980s, the supply of housing for the wealthy and for central government employees increased at a rapid pace, while housing for ordinary workers remained limited.

4. *The perception that wealth was acquired by illegitimate means.* At least into the 1980s, many Koreans found the display of wealth morally repugnant. Even many of the rich, who themselves acquired more goods than poorer people considered proper, criticized the display of wealth. The criticism was especially prominent among intellectuals and students, who felt that their intellectual achievements, based on meritocratic principles, entitled them to higher relative status than those businessmen who now enjoyed such a high standard of living. Many ordinary people believed that President Park had set a tone of a spartan style of living and was quick to crack down on officials and businessmen who engaged in flamboyant displays of wealth. It is widely believed that this spartan ethical tone essentially disappeared during the term of Chun Doo Hwan.

The possession of wealth by those in the highest income brackets raised more doubts about its legitimacy than in other newly industrializing countries. Unlike educational achievements, which required entrance examinations and were considered legitimate by an overwhelming portion of the population, the basis by which some people had acquired great wealth was not considered legitimate by large segments of society. There was a widespread perception that the availability of government aid to large companies in the form of low-interest loans, tax credits, and other arrangements provided a great help to the largest firms and that many of these special benefits were made on the basis of personal relationships. Although the precise facts on this accumulation of wealth are still not known, there have been enough revelations in the press to create strong convictions about the improper means by which the rich have achieved their wealth.

In contrast, the workers believed that they acquired their wages through long hours of sometimes tedious work and paid taxes accordingly. They believed that wealthy people who received income from the appreciation of stock and real estate often acquired their funds under dubious circumstances and did not pay taxes on their capital gains.

Prospects for a New Social Compact in Labor Relations

Although a social compact may not be as efficient and decisions may not be as quick as in the authoritarian system of the past, the new social pluralism and social demands of workers will eventually leave little choice. A social compact would provide a framework for resolving differences between management and labor with less disruption and tension than existed after 1986. Ideally a compact would be based on a workable legal framework, would encourage the professionalization of labor specialists in the government, enterprises, and unions, and would enable labor to have a positive voice in determining working conditions in exchange for exerting themselves on behalf of their company.

As of the early 1990s, the prospects for a social compact were not good. Many senior company officials were not yet convinced that such a compact was desirable. In their view it would constrain management prerogatives and grant more concessions to labor. The early authoritarian framework was so satisfactory from their point of view in containing labor demands and obtaining labor commitment that they still hoped to return to the early pattern of labor relationships—or at least a system as close to it as possible. Indeed, in Japan after three years of serious strikes from 1918 to 1921, leaders were able to reestablish a repressive system of labor discipline that lasted for twenty-five more years. Similarly in Korea, the labor crackdown in 1989–1990 not only greatly reduced labor disputes but led to only a modest rise in wages.

Many older company officials continued to bemoan the generation gap, believing that younger workers did not show proper respect and proper attitudes and that the problem was best handled by strict discipline. Many felt that the troubles essentially came from outside interference—radical students and intellectuals in the universities and secret conduits from the North or even from Japanese competitors. They bristled at the "extremism" and "communism" of intellectuals and labor leaders who, they alleged, wanted to bring down the whole capitalist system and stamp out all inequalities. When laborers resorted to violence, they felt they had no alternative but to use force to bring them under control. Many were convinced that the ordinary workers were pragmatic and concerned with stability. They believed that when workers saw that their companies really were in danger of failing in international competition, they would make the necessary concessions.

On the labor side, prospects were little better for labor leaders, who did not trust negotiations. Many labor leaders did not trust management and believed that they could improve their working conditions only by militant action. They believed that management could not be relied on to honor agreements and had too often been willing to resort to police and hired toughs to bring labor back in line. Many workers were convinced that any concession on their part would be taken as a sign of weakness and that negotiated concessions on the part of management would not later be honored. It followed, in their view, that they could represent their interests each year by first striking and then bargaining.

Labor's own leadership was also in disarray. There was tension between the FKTU and the new "democratic" union movement; far more troubling were the lack of consensus among labor activists and the inexperience of union leadership within individual enterprises. Rapid turnover in labor leadership was common in many of the new unions, and such turnover was not conducive to the establishment of orderly negotiations by labor representatives who could speak for their membership.

The inexperience of many labor leaders was partly a result of the government policy that prolonged repressive labor relations and stifled the development of government and company labor professionals and of independent labor leaders. The "gray hairs" in the union movement were almost exclusively associated with the FKTU and frequently, justly or unjustly, were not trusted by the rank and file. Yet younger leaders had at best limited experience with negotiations, and their knowledge of the broader picture of the Korean economy often was woefully inadequate. An attitude prevailed among some that strikes were not costly to workers, a view that was damaging to the economy and to workers' own interests in the long run.

Among labor leaders, employment security often was not a major concern. As of 1990, Korean workers had relatively little experience with employment dislocation due to cyclical factors, large business failures, automation, or the movement offshore of production facilities. Some believed that wage demands, even excessive ones, could be pressed because the government would not let a *chaebol* fail. Furthermore, the fact that nominal wage gains of 45 to 60 percent were granted from 1987 to 1989 reinforced the view that firms could afford to pay higher and higher wages. Such attitudes made it difficult for workers to achieve a consensus about feasible goals.

There is, however, room for some long-term optimism. Korea's economic growth has been characterized by a remarkable ability to adapt, and to adapt quickly. At different times, outside experts said the nation could neither build a competitive steel mill, nor successfully host the Olympics, nor hold direct elections for president—and the outside experts were proved wrong. Perhaps the Korean people will again confound the pessimists and arrive at a new understanding with labor in relatively few years. What may be most important is to gain a national consensus over the need for a new social compact: that neither the repressive character of the old system nor the chaos of the late 1980s will serve Korea.

A new labor relations framework cannot be achieved without the cooperation of the government. In response to requests by the United States for a democratic labor system, the Korean government in 1953 enacted a series of rules about labor relations that no one had planned to enforce and never were enforced. The government will have difficulty gaining credibility in the field of labor relations until the laws are brought closer in line with the government's actual policy. Although the proportion of strikes between 1987 and 1990 that have first gone through compulsory arbitration procedures has gone from zero to about one-fourth, the arbitration procedures must be simplified so that they are perceived as legitimate and followed in the vast majority of cases. To gain the compliance of labor in the new social compact, the government must both amend existing labor legislation and have an evenhanded enforcement procedure. The government will have to guarantee protection to workers and change laws that prevent workers from organizing their own workplaces. To gain labor support, government officials will have to be as strict with managers who violate rules by physically abusing workers, firing without cause, and not observing the labor code as it is with workers who violate rules about strikes.

Representatives from the government, management, and labor all lack experience in dealing with a labor force that is no longer compliant. In addition to mutual discussions required to gain consensus, there is a need for longer-term training programs for developing specialists to deal with labor-management issues.

Labor and management are beginning to confront new issues. Labor turnover has begun to decline, and workers are likely to become more interested in improving conditions where they work and in achieving long-range security. The age composition of workers is also changing, and management and workers must prepare for a situation when the overall wage burden to the company may be much greater. It is therefore important to achieve a social compact not only to deal with issues of labor strife that could be detrimental to all parties concerned, but also to begin to deal with fundamental long-range issues before they become acute.

For the past twenty-five years, the Korean economy has thrived under a labor system based on repression of labor's voice, and has relied on exit as labor's response to dissatisfaction with the workplace. Times have changed; the challenge that faces Korea is to be successful under a regime where labor is able to exercise its voice.

ACKNOWLEDGMENTS

This chapter is based in part on interviews conducted in Korea during the first two weeks of August 1989. We are indebted to many individuals for assistance in this research effort. We especially thank the following for making this research possible: Dr. Vincent Brandt, Dr. Choi Jang-Jip, Jeff Goldstein, Kim Byong-Kwan, Dr. Koo Bon-Ho, Dr. Lee Joung-Woo, Dr. Lee Sook-Jong, Dr. Park Fun-Koo, Dr. Park Young-Ki, Dr. Park Yung-Chul, Amy Rauenhorst, and Dr. Sung Ho-Keun.

NOTES

1. Labor disturbances contributed to annual nominal wage increases of 20 percent or more between 1988 and 1990. At the same time, hours lost to strikes and a generally contentious workplace environment hurt productivity growth. Taken together, and combined with an appreciation of the Korean *won*, unit labor costs (ULCs) in Korea rose by almost 70 percent between 1986 and 1990. By comparison, ULCs in Japan fell by

8 percent and in Taiwan rose by only 15 percent during this period. Barry Wilkinson, *Labour and Industry in the Asia Pacific* (Berlin: Walter de Gruyter, 1994), p. 91. These trends suggest a link between labor unrest and declining export competitiveness for Korean industry.

2. For a history of the Korean trade union movement, see Park Young-Ki, *Labor and Industrial Relations in Korea: System and Practice*, Institute for Labor and Management Studies 6 (Seoul: Sogang University Press, 1979).

3. The Special Law on National Security enacted in December 1971 placed the following limits on labor: (1) unions were required to secure government approval prior to engaging in collective negotiations; (2) when disputes arose; government intervention was automatic and its decisions final and binding; and (3) all strikes were prohibited. From Park Se-Il, "Labor Policy in Korea: Its Features and Problems" (paper presented at the Conference on the Role of the State in Economic Development, UCLA, August 1987).

4. Some authors, including Ronald Rodgers, "An Exclusionary Labor Regime Under Pressure: The Changes in Labor Relations in the Republic of Korea Since Mid-1987," *UCLA Pacific Basin Law Journal* 8, no. 1 (Spring 1990), place an equal emphasis on the economic as opposed to political goals of the authoritarian system of labor control. Rogers argues that the containment of labor costs was a primary objective of the Park regime's increasingly restrictive labor legislation. We, however, are more persuaded by Choi Jang-Jip, "A Corporatist Control of the Labor Union in South Korea," *Korean Social Science Journal* 2 (1985), and Choi Jang-Jip, *Labor and the Authoritarian State: Labor Unions in South Korean Manufacturing Industries, 1961–1980* (Seoul: Korean University Press, 1989), who notes, "The political designers of the junta wanted to secure the labor unions from any organized source of present or future opposition by preserving government sponsored leadership. They wanted also, *to a much lesser extent*, to see that labor would play a role that was at the very least not negative in implementation of the economic plans. The reason is relatively clear because, while political challenge by still active splinter groups was immediate, operational problems in managerial terms were very remote." Choi Jang-Jip, "Corporatist Control," p. 33 (emphasis added).

5. Korea's labor legislation, like that of Japan in the late 1940s, drew heavily on the U.S. Wagner Act of 1935 (which encouraged trade union independence) and other New Deal labor legislation.

6. The conventional wisdom that depicts unions as being detrimental to all but their members does not always stand up to careful scrutiny. At least for the United States, Richard B. Freeman and James Medoff, *What*

Do Unions Do? (New York: Basic Books, 1984), provide an exhaustive review of studies that assess the impact of unions on labor costs, employment, productivity, and other variables. They conclude, "On balance, unionization appears to improve rather than to harm the social and economic system. . . . Our analysis shows that unions are associated with greater efficiency in most settings, reduce overall earnings inequality, and contribute to, rather than detract from, economic and political freedom" (p. 19). The view that unions can, on net, benefit all participants in a nation's industrial labor relations system is defended for developing economies in the *1995 World Development Report, Workers in an Integrating World* (Washington, D.C.: World Bank, 1995), chap. 12.

7. Precise data on hours worked for Korea as well as other countries are difficult to obtain. In an independent study supported by the International Labour Organisation, Bai Moo-Ki, *Education, Workers' Behavior and Earnings: A Case Study of Manufacturing Workers in Korea* (Seoul: Institute of Economic Research, Seoul National University, August 1977), surveyed over one thousand manufacturing workers in the Seoul area and reported average workweeks of 60.7 hours compared to official data, which reported 52.5 hours for the same year.

8. Traditional values and ideology in Korea are considered in Vincent Brandt, "Korea," in George Lodge and Ezra Vogel, eds., *Ideology and National Competitiveness: An Analysis of Nine Countries* (Boston: Harvard Business School Press, 1987).

9. Like hours worked, turnover rates in Korea are high by international standards. Kim Soo-Kon, "Is the Japanese System of Lifetime Employment Applicable to a Developing Country Such As Korea?" (paper presented at Sixth World Congress of the International Industrial Relations Association, Kyoto, Japan, March 29–31, 1983), provides further discussion of turnover patterns in Korean firms.

10. The notion of exit versus voice options within human organizations is associated with the work of Albert O. Hirschmann, *Exit, Voice, and Loyalty* (Cambridge: Harvard University Press, 1971). The seminal application of the exit-voice model to labor organizations is Freeman and Medoff, *What Do Unions Do?* (See footnote 6.)

11. Mario Bognanno, *Korea's Industrial Relations at the Turning Point,* Korea Development Institute Working Paper 8816 (December 1988), argues a similar position and presents supporting empirical evidence; see especially Chart 1, p. 9.

12. By law, the new management-labor councils were not granted the right to negotiate wage agreements—evidence that the councils were not intended as a real departure from the existing system of labor control.

13. *New York Times,* November 22, 1970, p. 10.

14. To be precise, strikes increased precipitously on one occasion. From 1965 to 1984, officially recorded strikes amounted to roughly 100 per year, but in 1980 407 strikes were recorded by the Ministry of Labor. Strike activity in 1980, however, did not achieve the momentum that is discernible from 1985 onward.

15. Over a decade before, a strike had broken out in Ulsan at the Hyundai Shipyards. Construction on the shipyards began in 1972, and in 1974, frantically trying to meet orders for ships, the company had subcontracted out responsibility to a number of labor bosses. Worker amenities were sorely lacking, and workers under certain subcontractors, who had tougher working conditions and lower pay than other subcontract workers and still worse conditions than regular workers, rebelled. Some 3,000 went on strike.

16. As Park Young-Ki, "Economic Democratization and Industrial Relations in Korea with Special Reference to the Role of Unions" (paper presented at International Symposium on Economic Democracy and Industrial Relations, Seoul, Korea, June 16–17, 1988), has noted, a key difference in labor unrest before and after 1987 concerns both location and, perhaps more significant, firm size. After 1987 it is large enterprises, often members of the *chaebol,* that encountered violent and prolonged strikes.

17. The term *new "democratic" unions* is what Koreans, that is, those favorably disposed to these unions, called the new non-FKTU-affiliated unions. Our use of this term in no way implies that the new unions were either more or less democratic than the established FKTU unions. By way of contrast, many government officials, business leaders, and established trade unionists referred to the new unions as "radical" unions. However, when asked what was meant by this term, one leader of a new union replied that being a radical union implied loyalty to the workers, not an allegiance to any political ideology.

18. By 1989, 22 percent of South Korea's workers belonged to labor unions, according to statistics released by the Korean Labor Research Institute. As of December 31, 1988, some 1.71 million workers were labor union members. The figure represents an increase of 7.3 percent from June 1987, when President Chun Doo Hwan was still in power. The number of unions increased by 21.3 percent, to 6,142, during the same period. The Federation of Democratic Labor Unions, set up to oppose the traditional FKTU, had 770 affiliated unions with 200,000 paid-up members on its rolls—some 12 percent of all union members. *Korea Digest* 3, no. 2 (July 1989): 8.

19. Distribution data on Korea, whether on income or wealth, have long been subject to criticism. Studies have concluded that as many as 40 percent of Korean households, disproportionately drawn from the top- and bottom-income quintiles, have been excluded from surveys used to compute Korea's distribution of income. Analyses of the distribution of wealth have been even more handicapped by a lack of reliable data. One of the more thorough studies, Danny Leipziger et al., *The Distribution of Income and Wealth in Korea*, EDI Development Studies (Washington, D.C.: World Bank, 1992), concludes that Korea's distribution of wealth has become more unequal over time. This has certainly been true of landholdings. It is estimated that as of 1988 in Seoul, the top 10 percent of landowners owned 66 percent of the total. A similar pattern holds in other large cities. Since land prices rose by a factor of 14 between 1974 and 1989, three times as fast as the rise in real GNP, inequality in the distribution of real estate assets and in wealth overall must have increased. For further discussion see chapter 1.

7

Rural-Urban Disparity and Government Policies for Rural Development

Jong-Gie Kim and Jae-Young Son

Since the 1960s, the primary policy objective of Korea's national development has been to eliminate absolute poverty and to emerge as a middle-income nation through sustained and rapid economic growth. Although absolute standards of living improved dramatically over this period, not all regions and groups shared equally in the benefits of such remarkable growth. These imbalances took on the forms of rising inequality in the distribution of wealth and a widening disparity both between and within regions. Population and economic power became concentrated in large cities at the expense of smaller cities and rural areas. Seoul, the capital city, dominated other regions in the areas of politics, economics, culture, and education.

The need to pursue rapid economic growth as the primary policy objective was well understood by the Korean people. Regional imbalances were put aside temporarily as the goal of reducing the level of absolute poverty was fulfilled. However, with rising per capita incomes, problems of equity, relative poverty, and regional imbalances became growing social concerns. With further democratization unleashed by President Roh's June 29 Declaration, groups who did not perceive themselves as primary beneficiaries of the past growth strategy began making their voices heard. In the city, labor-management disputes over wages and working conditions became frequent. In the countryside, farmers concerned about the future of the rural economy and distrustful of the government began to demonstrate vigorously against agricultural policies.

The Korean government in the 1960s recognized the need for social development and undertook several policy initiatives to address the problems of high population concentration in Seoul and of rural development. But the effectiveness of these policies was limited by the scarcity of resources.

By the 1990s, endowed with more resources and facing greater political pressure, the Korean government started to pay more attention to areas of social development that were previously neglected.

The government's growing commitment to social development can be found in the series of five-year plans, with the first formal entry referring to social development in the Fourth Five Year Plan (1977–1981). The Fifth Five Year Plan (1982–1986), titled "Economic and Social Development," outlined three objectives: growth, equity, and the stability of society. The plan clearly defined the goal of social development by outlining the desire "to mitigate the undesired effects that have accumulated as part of the past growth process" and "to cope efficiently with the rising demands of the people for social welfare." The Sixth Five Year Plan (1987–1991) expanded on the notion of striking a balance between continued economic expansion and meeting the demands of different segments of society. In 1988, a presidential commission was formed to address the issues of economic restructuring and the shifting of national priorities. The commission called for a more balanced development strategy with the goals of higher living standards and improved social equity.

The Korean government faces new challenges as it attempts to become more integrated into the global economy and to correct for the imbalances resulting from its past development strategy, especially in the area of rural development. In order to understand these challenges, this chapter traces the pattern of regional population movements and examines the extent of urban-rural disparities. It also investigates the evolution of government programs to deal with regional imbalances.*

Regional Population Trends and Urban-Rural Disparity

Urban areas, especially Seoul, have experienced a rapid increase in population that has led to high rates of urbanization and a high concentration of population. Rural areas have experienced depopulation, due to massive rural-to-urban migration, mainly of young men (although the proportion of migrating young women has increased steadily). This migration was motivated by the superior living conditions of the city and by the better opportunity for employment and higher income.

Measures of employment, production, income, and consumption suggest that the disparity between rural and urban areas has narrowed some what since the 1970s. However, measures of infrastructure, which

* This chapter reviews the problems and policies as of 1990.

include both social and economic overhead capital, show that rural areas lagged far behind and did not catch up. These disparities are partially the result of the nature of the industrialization process and the development strategy pursued by the Korean government during earlier stages of growth.

Regional Population Trends

The Korean definition of an urban area is more restrictive than the U.S. definition, which counts people as urban residents if they live in a town of at least 2,500. In Korea, a municipality, or *Shi*, is defined as urban if there are at least 50,000 residents; this is similar to the U.S. requirement for a Standard Metropolitan Statistical Area (SMSA). In Korea, a *Shi* is a local government jurisdiction, whereas the U.S. SMSA includes not only the legal central city but also surrounding urbanized counties and suburbs. The Korean *Shi,* with the exception of Seoul, includes all residents in the general urban area.

A *Eup* (township) is an area with a municipal structure and a population between 20,000 and 50,000; a *Myon* (village) is classified as having under 20,000 inhabitants. A *Kun* is translated directly into English as a "county," but the meaning is different. In the United States a county can include a major metropolitan area, suburbs, and the surrounding rural area. The Korean *Kun* is an administrative area that includes residents living outside the *Shi*. Thus, a *Kun* can be used to describe residents living in rural areas. The *Shi* and the *Kun* are mutually exclusive, and the sum of the population living in the *Shi* and *Kun* is equal to the total population of the nation.

Table 7-1 identifies a few important features in regional population trends that characterize the period between 1960 and 1988.[1] The first is rapid urbanization. The population of *Shi* (cities) grew at an annual rate of 5.4 percent, raising the urbanization rate, defined as the percentage of the population living in urban areas, from 28 percent in 1970 to 74 percent in 1988. Second, the rural population declined. The population of *Kun* decreased at an annual rate of 1.8 percent, from over 18 million to about 11 million. Excluding *Eups*, townships with populations over 20,000, rural areas lost population at an annual rate of 2.6 percent. Third, there has been a high concentration of population in a few large urban areas. The six largest cities have accounted for an increasingly larger share of the total population.

Interregional population trends varied during the 1960–1988 period. The 1960s showed a marked concentration in Seoul. Later, new industrial cities, satellite cities around Seoul, and other major cities grew faster.[2]

Table 7-1. Regional Population Trends (1,000 persons)

	1960	1970	1980	1988	1960–1988
Total (*Shi* + *Kun*)	24,989	13,466	37,436	41,975	
		(1.89)	(1.53)	(1.24)	(1.87)
All *Shi* (cities)	6,997	12,953	21,434	30,922	
		(7.21)	(5.00)	(5.35)	(5.45)
Six largest cities	5,230	10,052	15,596	20,075	
		(8.22)	(4.41)	(3.05)	(4.92)
Seoul	2,445	5,536	8,364	10,287	
		(9.84)	(3.95)	(2.19)	(5.27)
All *Kun* (counties)	17,992	18,512	16,002	11,053	
		(-1.15)	(-2.23)	(-7.59)	(-1.73)
Eup (townships)	2,257	2,800	4,540	3,636	
		(1.48)	(4.05)	(-8.95)	(1.72)
Myon (villages)	15,731	15,372	11,463	7,417	
		(-2.17)	(-4.17)	(-6.89)	(-2.65)

Notes: Figures in parentheses indicate average annual rates of growth from the previous period. Inconsistencies among data sources are dealt with by giving priority to more recent years and by giving priority to the sources in the order listed. The definitions for a *Shi, Kun, Eup,* and *Myon* are in the text.
Sources: EPB, *Korea Statistical Yearbook* (1988); EPB, *Population and Housing Census* (1960, 1966, 1970, 1980); MHA, *Municipal Yearbook of Korea* (1971, 1989).

Although the population growth rate in Seoul has fallen below that of other cities since the 1970s, the share of Seoul's population in the national total steadily increased to almost a quarter of the national total (Table 7-2). The population of the six largest cities, including Seoul, also increased from 21 percent of the national total in 1960 to 48 percent in 1988, although the share of the six largest cities in the city total has been decreasing since the early 1970s.

The early 1970s seem to have been a watershed in regional population trends. Up to that year, urbanization had been accelerating, marked by explosive population growth in Seoul. After the mid-1970s, the pace of urbanization slowed, and the share of Seoul and other major cities in

Table 7-2. Population Concentration (percentages)

	1960	1970	1980	1988
All *Shi* (cities)	28.0	41.2	57.3	73.7
Six largest cities	20.9	31.9	41.7	47.8
Seoul	9.8	17.6	22.3	24.5
All *Kun* (counties)	72.0	58.8	42.7	26.3
All *Eup* (townships)	9.0	8.9	12.1	8.7
All *Myon* (villages)	63.0	48.9	30.6	17.7
Out of *Shi* total				
Six largest cities	74.7	77.6	72.8	64.9
Seoul	34.9	42.7	39.0	33.3

Source: See Table 7-1 sources.

Table 7-3. Distribution of Urban Population by City Size

City Population	1960 Number of Cities	%	1970 Number of Cities	%	1980 Number of Cities	%	1985 Number of Cities	%
Over 1 million	2	51.6	3	65.6	4	66.3	4	62.7
500,000–1 million	1	9.7	1	5.0	2	6.4	3	8.8
250,000–500,000	2	10.2	3	9.1	7	11.0	8	12.0
100,000–250,000	4	10.1	11	11.8	21	14.2	21	12.7
Less than 100,000	18	18.5	14	8.5	6	2.1	14	3.9
Total	27	100.0	32	100.0	40	100.0	50	100.0

Note: Urban population refers to the residents in Korean municipalities with at least 50,000 residents.
Source: Kwon Won-Young, "Regional Development Policies and Strategies for the Sixth Economic and Social Development Plan," in Hwang Myong-Chan and Harry Richardson, eds., *Urban and Regional Policy in Korea and International Experiences* (Seoul: Kon-Kuk University Press, 1987), reproduced with permission.

the total urban population decreased as medium and small cities grew faster (Table 7-3). Most of Korea's fast-growing cities are located in either the capital region or along the Seoul-Pusan axis, the center of industrial development.

Rural population grew more slowly than the national average after 1960, and actually began to decrease in the late 1960s. Within *Kuns*, *Eups* (towns) grew faster than the national average (with the exception of the 1966–1970 period). This means that *Myon* (villages) experienced rapid depopulation, and the rate of loss accelerated from –2.17 percent in the 1960s to –6.89 percent in the 1980s (see Table 7-1). Accordingly, the share of *Kun* in the total national population fell from 72 percent in 1960 to 26 percent in 1988, and the share of *Myon* population from 63 percent to 18 percent (see Table 7-2).

Migration
Rapid urbanization implies massive rural-to-urban migration. Table 7-4 shows that between 1965 and 1970, 11 percent of all males and a similar percentage of females moved to other provinces. The capital region (Seoul, Inchon, and Kyonggi) and Pusan gained population by net migration, while *all* other provinces lost population. From 1970 to 1980, with the exception of the island of Cheju and autonomous cities other than Seoul and Pusan, a similar trend occurred. Table 7-5 shows that the contribution of migration to urban population growth is usually more or less similar to that of natural growth, but during the latter half of the 1960s, migration accounted for around 75 percent of growth, with natural growth explaining the rest.

Table 7-4. Five-Year Male Net Migration Rate by Province (percentage)

	1965–70	1970–75	1975–80
Seoul City/Province	27.84	11.12	11.91
Inchon	—	—	23.19
Kyonggi	1.35	8.57	9.20
Pusan City	17.74	15.12	16.71
South Kyongsang Province	-10.67	-3.88	-5.56
Taegu City	—	—	13.60
North Kyongsang Province	-5.86	-2.02	-10.82
Kangwon Province	-6.36	-9.72	-10.25
North Chungchong Province	-12.42	-5.12	-11.22
South Chungchong Province	-9.88	-5.29	-6.20
North Cholla Province	-12.42	-5.12	-11.22
South Cholla Province	-9.99	-9.03	-11.32
Cheju Province	-0.89	0.17	4.68
Total net interprovince migrants (1,000 persons)	1,652	1,203	1,910
Ratio to total population	11.25	7.62	10.95

Notes: The figures concern male migration, but female migration rates are not significantly different.
Five-year net migration rate = Five-year net in-migration / Total population of province. A positive value indicates net in-migration. A negative value indicates net out-migration.
Source: Chung Young-Il, "An Analysis of Migration by the Census Data," in H.I. Choi, Y.I. Chung, and Y.C. Byun, eds., *Migration and Socioeconomic Developments* (Seoul: KIPH and EPB, 1986), reproduced with permission.

Table 7-5. Components of Urban Population Growth, 1960–1980

	1960–1966	1966–1970	1970–1975	1975–1980
Total urban population growth (1,000)	2,709	3,223	3,842	4,638
Components of urban population growth (%)				
Gaining *Shi* (city) status	8.0	—	5.2	10.5
Annexation	9.3	—	2.5	4.1
Net migration	40.6	73.2	45.1	39.7
Natural growth	42.1	26.8	47.2	45.7

Source: Hwang Myung–Chan and Jin–Ho Choi, "Evolution of the Settlement System in Korea," in Hwang and Richardson, *Urban and Regional Policy.*

Regional Disparity (with Emphasis on Urban-Rural Disparity)

Employment. Exports have been the engine of national economic growth, and the manufacturing sector is at the heart of export activity. In 1960, manufacturing accounted for 7.5 percent of total employment and 14 percent of production, but by 1985, the ratios had gone up to 24 percent and 30 percent, respectively. In the twenty-five-year period, manufacturing employment grew at an annual average rate of 7.8 percent. This fast growth was not achieved uniformly throughout the country. Table 7-6 breaks down the growth of manufacturing sectors by region. During the 1970s, annual average rates of increase in number of firms

Table 7-6. Growth of the Manufacturing Sector

	1971		1980		1988	
	Firms	Employment	Firms	Employment	Firms	Employment
Nation	23.4	848.2	30.8	2,014.8	50.1	2,738.4
			(3.1)	(10.1)	(8.4)	(52)
All *Shi* (cities)	12.7	606.8	25.2	1,725.4	37.9	2,177.3
			(7.89)	(12.3)	(7.0)	(3.9)
All *Kun* (counties)	10.7	241.4	5.6	289.4	12.2	561.0
			(-6.94)	(2.0)	(13.9)	(11.7)
Seoul-Pusan axis	14.5	671.9	23.8	1,803.7	42.2	2,451.8
			(5.6)	(11.6)	(10.0)	(5.2)
All other regions	8.9	176.3	7.0	211.1	7.9	286.6
			(-2.6)	(2.0)	(2.0)	(5.2)

Notes: Units of measurement: 1,000 establishments and 1,000 persons. Figures in the parentheses indicate percentage average annual rate of growth from the previous period.
Sources: EPB, *Korea Statistical Yearbook* (1973, 1982, 1988); MHA, *Municipal Yearbook of Korea* (1972, 1981, 1989); City of Taegu, *Taegu Statistical Yearbook* (1972).

and employment growth were 7.9 percent and 12.3 percent, respectively, in the *Shi* (cities), but –6.9 percent and 2.0 percent in the *Kuns* (counties). This sharp contrast seems to have been reversed in the early 1980s. Nonetheless, the manufacturing sector remains concentrated along the Seoul-Pusan axis. From 1971 to 1988, the share of manufacturing employment in the Seoul-Pusan axis rose from 79 percent to 90 percent, and the number of firms from 62 percent to 84 percent (Table 7-7).

Among cities, Seoul's dominance in manufacturing employment was declining, with manufacturing employment growing faster in medium and small cities than in major cities. Manufacturing employment in Seoul as a share of manufacturing employment in all cities declined steadily from 46 percent in 1971 to 25 percent in 1988. Medium and small cities

Table 7-7. Concentration of the Manufacturing Sector (percentage)

	1971		1980		1988	
	Firms	Employees	Firms	Employees	Firms	Employees
All *Shi*	54.4	71.5	81.9	85.6	75.6	79.5
Six largest cities	38.7	58.0	57.3	57.9	57.9	51.5
All other cities	15.7	13.6	24.6	27.8	17.8	28.0
All *Kun*	45.6	28.5	18.1	14.4	24.4	20.5
Seoul-Pusan axis	62.0	79.2	77.2	89.5	84.3	89.5
All other regions	38.0	20.8	22.8	10.5	15.7	10.5
Six largest cities	71.1	81.0	69.9	67.6	76.5	64.7
Seoul	43.9	45.9	30.3	25.8	40.3	24.8
All other cities	28.9	19.0	30.1	32.4	23.5	35.3

Source: See sources for Table 7- 6.

increased their share of manufacturing employment over the same time period from 19 percent to 35 percent. New firms were more concentrated in Seoul and other major cities, and lent support to the claim that maintaining the vitality of large cities was important for the growth of new firms. Large cities served as incubators for new firms because of the advantages they offered: easier access to the latest technology, quicker and more efficient communications, economies-of-scale associated with larger markets, and closer proximity of exchange. Typically these new firms started out small, with usually no more than five persons. As they expanded in size and in number of employees, they tended to move out of the city, where the high price of real estate prevented them from expanding or moving to a larger establishment. This pattern of small firms' starting in the city and then, as they grew, moving out of the city explains the discrepancy in the number of firms and employment between the *Shi* and the *Kun*. Large cities experienced faster growth rates in the number of firms, but the countryside typically had faster employment growth because expanding firms relocated outside the city.

Income. Comprehensive and reliable data for interregional income distribution are difficult to find, but a range of indicators suggests some conclusions. One such indicator is gross regional product (GRP), a measure of regional income, not of production. The larger the interregional flow of factor income or the greater the amount of transfer income, including capital gains, the less relevant GRP is as an indicator of regional income disparity. There are many concerns about the accuracy of Korean GRP data,[3] and they should be interpreted with caution. Table 7-8, reproduced from a World Bank study, indicates that regional income disparity grew in the 1960s but decreased after the 1970s.[4] The coefficient of variation of GRP decreased from 0.37 in 1967 to 0.22 by 1983, and the ratio of highest to lowest GRP from over 3 to about 1.8. According to these GRP estimates, the largest beneficiary of Korea's economic growth policy was South Kyongsang Province, which contained a number of important new industrial estates. South and North Cholla provinces lagged far behind.

Table 7-9 compares differences between farm household incomes and urban wage earner household incomes. Compiled by several agencies using different methods, these two series are not entirely comparable, but they suggest that the income disparity between the farm household and the urban wage earner household has decreased.[5] Table 7-9 suggests that the average monthly income of farm households caught up to that of urban wage earner households by 1973, and afterward even exceeded it (with a few exceptions). However, it is dangerous to conclude that the

Table 7-8. Per Capita Gross Regional Product by Province (Lowest GRP=100)

	1963	1967	1978	1983
Seoul	220	303	170	179
Kyonggi	131	150	148	147
North Kyongsang	114	130	113	130
Pusan	174	247	150	144
South Kyongsang	*100*	132	163	173
Kangwon	115	142	104	118
North Chungchong	114	137	114	118
South Chungchong	119	134	102	108
North Cholla	123	117	*100*	*100*
South Cholla	104	*100*	102	117
Cheju	108	133	111	119
Coefficient of variation	0.27	0.37	0.22	0.22

Source: World Bank, *Korea: Spatial Strategy Review* (Washington, D.C.: World Bank, 1986).

income differential of average rural and urban households disappeared or even reversed itself after the early 1970s. Household income data have several problems. We list four here.

First, there is disagreement as to whether changes in the value of grain inventories due to changes in price should be included in farm household income since an increase in the value of these inventories may merely reflect the increase in the price of grain. Annual price inflation for foodstuffs between 1970 and 1987 averaged around 13 percent. Thus the presence of inventories bias rural farm household incomes upward. Some economists have computed revised estimates of farm household income that take into account this "undue" capital gain; their estimates adjust rural incomes downward.[6]

Second, these surveys exclude a significant proportion of the household population—at least 39 percent of the total population according to some estimates.[7] Excluded from both data series are self-employed

Table 7-9. Rural Farm Household versus Urban Wage Earner Household Income (1,000 *won* per month)

	1965	1970	1975	1980	1985	1987
Urban wage earner households	9.4	28.2	65.5	234.1	431.2	561.7
Rural farm households	9.4	21.3	72.7	224.4	478.0	544.6
Rural/urban (percentage)	100	76	111	96	111	97

Notes: Original urban household data series were compiled by EPB, *Family Income and Expenditure Survey*, and rural data by Ministry of Agriculture, Fishery and Forestry, *Farm Household Income Survey*.
Source: EPB, *Social Indicators in Korea* (1988).

business owners (including medical doctors, lawyers, and private businessmen), an important urban high-income class, and nonfarm households in rural areas, a relatively poor group in the rural population. This results in biasing downward the urban household income level and biasing upward the rural household income level.

Third, the household surveys include property income in their urban household calculations but not for rural households. Property income plays a much larger role in urban household income than in rural household income. In 1984, property income—income from owner-occupied or yearly rent deposit housing—represented 23 percent of the income for urban households in Korea. The exclusion of property income from rural household income biases rural household income downward.

Fourth, these income figures need to be deflated by some appropriate price indexes that reflect the differences in the cost of living and patterns of lifestyle between urban and rural dwellers. In 1974, it has been estimated, the cost of living for urban residents was 19.4 percent higher.[8]

Conclusions on income disparity based on these income surveys are not wholly reliable since the direction and degree of bias are unclear. Choo looked at the urban-rural income differential and, by making adjustments to the data in order to make them more comparable, computed an "effective level of disposable income" that accounts for differences in cost of living, household size, and tax burdens between rural and urban areas.[9] His results confirm the general trend as shown by the original income surveys: the rural-urban income disparity had narrowed by the end of the 1970s (Table 7-10).

Social and Economic Infrastructure. From the regional development perspective, infrastructure can be divided into two main categories. The first, economic overhead capital, provides opportunities for employment and income by attracting capital investments; the second, social overhead capital, improves the quality of life of the population.[10]

Table 7-10. Effective Level of Disposable Income: Rural Farm Households versus Urban Wage Earners Household (1,000 *won*)

	1965	1970	1975	1979
Urban household	109.6	361.4	838.8	2573.8
Rural household	114.1	277.3	958.3	2369.9
Rural/urban (percentage)	104.1	76.7	114.3	92.1

Notes: See the text for the definition of effective level of disposable income.
Source: Choo Hak-Chung, *Widening Urban Rural Income Differentials in Korea: A Re-examination*, KDI Working Paper 8205 (August 1982), p.24, reproduced with permission.

ECONOMIC OVERHEAD CAPITAL. Construction of industrial estates has been a symbol of the nation's determination to industrialize. Large-scale national industrial estates, intended for brand-new heavy industry, were developed primarily in the 1970s in areas with little existing manufacturing base. Many of them were built in the southeastern part of the country in order to exploit geographic advantages in the international flow of raw materials and products, but some were built near Seoul to accommodate factories moving out of the city. Their location also reflected the government's concern over excessive industrial concentration in Seoul. Estates were intended to be magnets drawing employment and population out of the capital city. Local industrial estates usually grew out of the existing manufacturing base of cities, where light industrial factories were located. Table 7-11 shows that in terms of area, number of factories, and employment, over 70 percent of all industrial estates were constructed along the Seoul-Pusan axis and few in other regions.

Accessibility is important for both business activities and living standards. The amount of paved road increased remarkably nationwide, but the disparity between rural and urban areas remained large. Table 7-12 shows that between 1971 and 1989, the percentage of roads paved increased in both the cities and the countryside, but priority was given to linkage between Seoul, Pusan, and other major industrial centers. Rural areas still had a relatively low pavement ratio at the end of the 1980s.[11]

In terms of other measures of public services availability, such as water, sewer, garbage collection, and telephone services, large gaps existed between *Shi* (city) and *Eup* (town), and the gap did not narrow (Table 7-13). Such services were virtually nonexistent in *Myon* (village).

Table 7-11. Distribution of Industrial Estates, 1987

	Factory Sites Sold[a] (1,000 m)	Firms (establishments)	Employment (1,000 persons)
Seoul-Pusan axis total	144,936	13,338	1,313.4
National government estates	123,355	8,874	946.7
Local industrial estates	7,399	644	59.9
Private	14,242	3,820	306.8
Other regions total	23,263	766	60.9
National government estates	14,424	103	12.2
Local industrial estates	8,839	663	48.7

[a] Total of factory sites includes only areas intended for sale. It may be smaller than the total area actually developed as industrial estates.
Source: Ministry of Commerce and Trade, *Industrial Estates* (1988).

Table 7-12. Road Statistics: Pavement Ratios between *Shi* and *Kun*
(percentages)

Year	*Shi* (Cities)	*Kun* (Counties)
1971	14.2	7.5
1975	40.8	14.4
1980	56.1	18.9
1985	67.1	36.4
1989	74.8	46.6

Note: The pavement ratio is the paved road length divided by the total road length.
Source: Ministry of Construction, *Construction Yearbook* (1971, 1975, 1980, 1985, 1989).

SOCIAL OVERHEAD CAPITAL. In many respects, housing conditions were better in rural areas than in urban areas. Table 7-14 shows that between rural and urban areas, the home ownership rate was higher in the countryside, the floor space per household larger, the number of households per housing unit smaller, the number of people per room smaller, room size larger, and housing expenditure in total expenditure smaller.[12] This picture of better housing conditions in rural areas is reversed if we consider differences in housing quality (Table 7-15). Rural houses in the 1980s were generally equipped with traditional dirt-floor kitchens, and few had flush toilets or separate spaces for bathing. Many rural households used firewood for cooking and heating.

Education is traditionally important in any Korean family's decisions for the present and future. The goal of primary and secondary education in Korea is admission to one of a handful of good universities in Seoul. With such a single universal goal of education, it could be easy to define

Table 7-13. Selected Public Services

		Water[a] (%)	Sewer[b] (%)	Garbage Collection[c] (%)	Telephone (lines/100 persons) (%)
1971	*Shi*	79.1	—	84.1	4.1
	Eup	41.9	—	—	1.7
1975	*Shi*	81.0	—	75.7	6.4
	Eup	44.0	—	52.6	3.5
1980	*Shi*	89.7	53.2	94.0	10.3
	Eup	66.8	47.3	55.5	6.6
1985	*Shi*	90.5	83.0	96.7	18.8
	Eup	51.1	59.8	61.1	17.4
1988	*Shi*	92.1	88.5	96.8	27.3
	Eup	55.7	61.5	64.0	23.2

[a]Households with water services/Total households.
[b]People in sewer service area/Population.
[c]People in cleaning service area/Population.
Source: Ministry of Home Affairs, *Municipal Yearbook* (1971, 1975, 1980, 1985, 1988).

Table 7-14. Housing Conditions

	1970		1975		1980		1985	
	Shi	*Kun*	*Shi*	*Kun*	*Shi*	*Kun*	*Shi*	*Kun*
Housing supply ratio[a] (percentage)	58.8	92.6	56.9	91.8	56.6	91.7	54.1	87.8
Floor space per housing unit (m^2)	50.4	46.4	65.6	53.5	77.3	60.7	82.3	57.2
Floor space per household (m^2)	27.1	41.4	35.8	47.2	41.1	52.5	43.6	48.6
Percentage of housing units occupied by one household	55.2	91.1	51.6	90.0	51.1	89.8	53.8	89.1
Number of people per room	2.7	2.2	2.5	2.1	2.2	1.9	1.9	1.7

[a] **Number of housing units/Number of households.**
Source: EPB, *Social Indicators in Korea* (1988).

the output measure of education of a region: the number of students who pass the entrance examinations of a few universities. However, such data are not available. Table 7-16 shows the ratio of high school graduates who were admitted to any four-year university. *Shi* high schools consistently performed better, although the gap decreased after the mid-1970s.

Table 7-15. Auxiliary Housing Facilities, 1985 (percentages)

	Shi	*Kun*
Kitchen		
Western style	54.9	9.8
Traditional style	45.1	90.2
Bathroom		
Hot and cold water	32.8	4.4
Cold water only	20.2	6.5
No room for bathing	47.0	89.1
Toilet		
Flush	54.4	7.2
Nonflush	45.6	92.8
Type of fuel used for cooking		
Coal briquet	51.5	41.8
Gas	35.0	9.5
Firewood	0.9	41.7
Oil	11.1	2.5
Electricity	1.2	1.9
Others	0.3	2.6
Type of fuel used for heating		
Coal briquet	85.6	46.2
Oil/central heating	11.7	1.0
Firewood	1.9	52.6
Others	0.8	0.2

Source: EPB, *Social Indicators in Korea* (1988).

Table 7-16. High School Graduates Admitted to Four-Year Universities
(percentages)

	1971	1975	1980	1985	1987
(A) *Shi* (cities)	34.04	33.51	37.54	40.76	39.35
(B) *Eup* (townships)	22.73	16.75	23.16	29.13	28.16
A-B	11.31	16.76	14.38	11.63	11.19

Note: Ratio to total high school graduates.
Source: MHA, *Municipal Yearbook of Korea* (1971, 1975, 1980, 1985, 1987).

On the input side of education, it is hard to find evidence for regional disparity in favor of urban schools. Small-city and rural-area schools had smaller classes, better teacher to student ratios, larger building and land areas, and larger government subsidies per student. Unless the quality of such items and other factors (for example, quality of teachers, competition among students, parental concern, and resources for education) could be measured, it is not possible to draw conclusions about any disparity of educational inputs.

Among rural households, lack of access to medical service ranked first in a survey concerning inconveniences in life.[13] Table 7-17 shows that the concentration of medical facilities and personnel increased steadily in cities. In terms of quality, the disparity became even greater than these figures suggest, since physicians who acquired better training in the top medical schools in Seoul and a few other cities tended to stay in those cities; furthermore, advanced medical equipment was found only in the largest hospitals, located in the cities.

Although measures of income disparity suggest that the gap between rural and urban areas narrowed after the 1960s, other measures tell a different story. Since most industrial estates were planned and supported by the government, manufacturing industries tended to concentrate in

Table 7-17. Concentration of Medical Facilities and Personnel in Cities
(percentages)

	1971	1975	1980	1985	1987
General hospitals	77.5	83.9	89.9	90.8	94.8
Other hospitals	72.5	66.9	91.6	86.4	82.7
Clinics	72.2	75.9	80.4	86.1	86.9
Dental clinics	85.3	87.5	90.2	90.8	90.7
Physicians	69.4	81.1	67.4	91.6	92.7
Dentists	79.7	81.0	75.4	92.0	92.8

Note: *Shi* total/(*Shi* total + *Eup* total); otherwise, (*Shi* total/National total).
Sources: MHA, *Municipal Yearbook of Korea* (1971, 1975, 1980, 1985, 1987); MHSA, *Health and Social Statistics Yearbook* (1971, 1975, 1980, 1985, 1987).

the cities along the Seoul-Pusan axis. Broad measures of social and economic infrastructure suggest a similar trend. Indicators of economic infrastructure such as paved roads, telephone, water, and sewer services show that the gap between the city and the countryside was large and widened. Social infrastructure indicators such as housing and educational and medical facilities offer further support of a persistent gap.

Overview of Spatial Policies

Concerns About Regional Population Trend

Government policies, whether tagged as spatial or not, affect the location decisions of population and industry. Nonspatial or sector policies were more responsible for the high economic and population concentration in Seoul, and the decline of rural areas, than any space-specific policies. A high degree of urbanization, especially concentration in one major city, is not peculiar to Korea. Other countries have gone through similar stages of concentration and centralization, followed by decentralization and later deconcentration. Only the unusual speed of the process is unique to Korea, reflecting the nation's fast economic growth.

Korea's national growth strategy made population concentration inevitable, and growth objectives probably could not have been achieved without exploiting the agglomerated urban economies. Millions of migrants supplied abundant labor to the development process while also improving their own living conditions. The changing population distribution made a great contribution to fast economic growth and to spreading the benefits of growth among a larger part of the population. Nevertheless, the government decided that a more balanced regional population profile was desired.[14] Four major concerns, which have justified most spatial policies since the mid-1960s, can be identified.

The first major concern was national security. Korea was, and still is, technically at war with North Korea, and high tension still exists along the demilitarized zone just fifty kilometers away from Seoul. The government worried that concentration of population and economic activity in the capital made the nation vulnerable to a surprise attack and that emergency relocation would be impossible if the need were to arise.

Second, Seoul, and later other major cities, had difficulty coping with the rapid influx of migrants since the mid-1960s. Housing shortages, rapidly increasing property prices, traffic congestion, strain on the social and physical infrastructure, and concentration of the urban poor were hard to deal with under the constraints of limited economic and administrative resources.

The third concern was the effect of out-migration on population-losing regions. Some worried about the instability of rural family structure, others about the future of agriculture, and still others about the lack of young women, a mobile segment of the population, to marry farmers. Maintaining the traditional family farming system, however, was neither desirable nor realistic. As industrialization progressed, agriculture increasingly had to be run like a business, and rural household income needed to diversify to include more off-farm sources.

The last and most politically sensitive issue was the geographic concentration of growing cities along the Seoul-Pusan axis and the loss of population in the southwestern part of the nation. Although Korea remains physically divided between the North and the South, regional antipathy has also divided the nation between the East and the West. Partly due to Korea's long tradition of valuing community ties, there has been a great deal of distrust and friction between Koreans of the southeast Kyongsong region and those of the southwest Cholla region—the native regions of the two opposing political parties of the 1980s. At times, these regional conflicts dominated all other political issues.

The focus of Korean development policy on the growth of cities along the Seoul-Pusan axis caused some resentment among the residents of regions that were left behind. It is not clear whether economic efficiency dictated such a locational pattern, but the loss of population and the relative decline of the southwest region have been sources of much regional conflict.

Spatial Policies in the 1970s
A 1964 cabinet resolution attempted to control the excessive growth of Seoul by relocating secondary government agencies to other cities, discouraging new industrial development in Seoul, developing satellite cities and new industrial cities, and setting up educational and cultural facilities in local areas. The strategy of pushing population and economic activities out of Seoul and attracting them to less developed regions was reaffirmed in spatial policy statements after 1964. However, effective policies were difficult to formulate, and a detailed system of regulations and incentives was developed slowly. These measures included the construction of the Seoul-Pusan Expressway and industrial complexes in Ulsan and Pohang, new or higher taxes on residents or manufacturing establishments in Seoul and other large cities, stricter land use regulations, restrictions on the expansion of educational institutions, incentives for

relocation out of the Seoul region, and occasional organizational changes in the government.[15]

By 1970, it was clear that these piecemeal measures were not enough to counteract growing concentration. A comprehensive plan was called for to define policy objectives and strategy, assess resource requirements and the impact of policy measures, and coordinate the policies of different ministries. The First National Physical Development Plan (1972–1981) was drawn up to meet this need.[16] Adopting the growth pole concept, this plan intended to draw population out of Seoul and other large cities by developing large industrial complexes far away from Seoul and relatively small local industrial estates around the country. However, this plan was subordinate to the five-year economic development plans, and investments were made only when the proposed projects coincided with overall economic growth goals. Essentially the plan served as an infrastructure investment section of the economic development plans, despite its professed goal of balanced regional growth.

The First National Physical Development Plan established the Seoul-Pusan, Seoul-Kwangju, Seoul-Kangnung, and Pusan-Sunchun express-ways, the first line of the Seoul subway system, electrification of the Chungang Railroad Line, and several multipurpose dams. On the regional development side, new industrial cities like Changwon and Yeochun were constructed, and Ulsan, Pohang, and Masan were expanded. Seoul's growth was restricted, and surrounding areas beyond the green belt began to grow quickly. These projects, however, were not very effective in slowing the rate of concentration. New industrial cities, filled with massive factories, lacked social amenities. Suburban areas of Seoul did not develop on their own; they served mainly as factory sites for Seoul business firms and provided cheaper housing for Seoul commuters.[17]

Spatial Policies in the 1980s
By the beginning of the 1980s, researchers and policymakers began to think that the strategy of building regional employment bases and moving people to jobs was too costly if the direct or indirect costs of infrastructure construction were borne by the residents of these growing cities. This assessment was reflected in the Second National Physical Development Plan (1982–1991). The objectives were the same as those of the first plan: controlling the growth of major cities, especially Seoul, and improving the distribution of population and of economic activity. The approach differed, however; instead of constructing massive industrial complexes designed to attract residents out of Seoul and other major cities, the plan

aimed at maintaining rural and small city populations by providing better living conditions and employment opportunities.

Twenty-eight integrated service delivery areas and induced growth centers were designated. Three primary growth centers (Taegu, Kwangju, and Taejon) and twelve secondary growth centers were chosen to provide managerial leadership and employment services. The locations of these centers reflected the goal of spurring growth in the stagnant regions outside the Seoul-Pusan axis. This strategy called for incentives to attract manufacturing establishments to these growth centers, the relocation of educational and other service facilities, the improvement of transportation around and between growth centers, and the delegation to local governments of administrative power and the means to finance public and private investment in the growth centers.

Most of these measures could not be implemented as planned because of conflicts with other policy goals. Since the goal of national economic growth dominated the goal of correcting regional disparity, limited investment resources were reserved for the latter. This order of priority began to change slowly, and in the mid-1980s the Sixth Economic and Social Development Plan (1987–1991) paid serious consideration to regional policy goals. The Second National Physical Plan was revised accordingly. For the first time, regional policy objectives were accorded the same importance as growth in the gross national product (GNP), and coordinated government efforts were directed toward achieving them.

In the revised Second National Physical Development Plan, regional economic clusters replaced integrated service delivery areas and induced growth centers as the units of regional planning. Regional clusters were the urban areas surrounding six central cities (Seoul, Pusan, Taegu, Kwangju, Taejon, and Kangnung).[18] The central cities were to play the same role in their surrounding areas as Seoul had played for the whole nation. In order to reduce their dependence on Seoul, each regional economic cluster would have its own administrative infrastructure for international trade, high-technology industrial parks and telecommunication facilities, commodity distribution centers, public transportation, and urban express networks. The clusters were to become the instruments for "regionalizing national plans."[19]

Rural Development and Agricultural Policies in the 1970s

Reducing regional disparities in income, employment, living conditions, and infrastructure provision has been shaped by market forces and sectoral policies and, in the case of rural development, by agricultural policies. The dual price system for agricultural products, the Saemaul Undong (New Community Movement) and the Saemaul factories are three policies important to the study of rural development.

Dual Price System for Agricultural Products

After the Korean War (1950–1953), Korea could not meet its domestic demand for food grains—most importantly, rice—without outside help. The reconstruction of the nation's cities and industries was considered more important than supporting the rural economy; thus, the government relied on U.S. foreign aid to keep the government purchase price below the market price.[20] Although low food prices contributed to industrial development and mitigated inflationary pressure during the 1960s, they hurt the farm economy and increased dependence on foreign supply. In the late 1960s, as U.S. foreign aid dwindled, Korea was forced to pay hard currency for its food imports (Table 7-18). The increasing need for foreign currency, coupled with the widening differential in income between cities and rural areas, forced the government to change its grain price policy. It raised the purchase price of food grain to encourage production and increase farm income. The government feared, however, that high food prices would be a burden on the urban lower-income classes and would add to inflationary pressure in the economy.

The solution to this dilemma was the introduction of a dual price system for rice and barley. Starting in 1969, the government bought grain crops at certain prices and sold them at lower ones. Table 7-19 shows the estimated production cost of rice, the government purchase price,

Table 7-18. Self-Sufficiency Ratio and Imports of Major Crops

Year	Rice		All Grain Crops[a]	
	Ratio (percentage)	Imports (US$ millions)	Ratio (percentage)	Imports (US$ millions)
1965	100.9	—	65	43
1970	93.1	88	70	202
1975	94.6	202	75	722
1977	103.4	—	77	517
1979	85.7	164	79	952
1981	66.2	1,139	81	2,181
1983	97.6	66	83	1,208
1985	103.3	—	85	1,126
1988	97.9	—	88	1,448

[a]Rice, barley, wheat, and corn.
Note: The self-sufficiency ratio is the percentage of consumption demand supplied by domestic production.
Source: MAFF, *Major Statistics of A.F.F.* (1989).

Table 7-19. Dual Price System for Rice (*Won*/80 kg)

	A	B	C	D	E	C/(B + E)
Year	Production Cost	Government Purchase Price	Government Sale Price	Market Price	Operating Expenses	Breakeven Ratio (%)
1970	4,160	5,151	5,400	6,106	577	0.94
1973	6,075	9,888	9,500	10,204	792	0.89
1975	11,045	15,760	13,000	18,653	1,488	0.75
1977	14,400	23,200	19,500	24,843	2,424	0.76
1979	22,151	30,000	26,500	37,787	5,088	0.76
1981	34,263	45,750	44,000	55,584	9,750	0.79
1983	41,166	55,970	52,280	58,827	9,358	0.80
1985	44,235	57,650	54,260	55,971	16,262	0.73
1987	50,988	64,160	55,120	74,666	16,800	0.68
1988	53,750	73,140	49,610	83,200	13,360	0.57

Sources: MAFF, *Statistical Yearbook of A.F.F.* (1988), and *Major Statistics of A.F.F.* (1989).

the actual sale price of the government's rice supply, the market price, and goverment's operating expense. The government's sale price was consistently lower than the market price, and the gap between the government purchasing price and the breakeven point (the difference between the government sale price and the sum of the government purchase price and operating expenses) grew, and a mounting deficit in the Grain Management Fund was created. Since this deficit was largely financed by borrowing from the central bank (Table 7-20), the extra money needed to finance the deficit became a major constraint on the country's economic management.[21]

Apart from the macroeconomic concern about inflation, the following question can be raised from a regional policy perspective: Can an artificially high grain price generate a healthy rural economy? The agricultural sector still consisted of small-scale family farming, and there

Table 7-20. Deficits in the Grain Management Fund and Funding Sources (billion *won*)

	Five-Year Total	Rice	Barley	Other Grains	Others*	General Account Subsidy	Net Borrowing
1971–1975	246.2	38.1	77.0	4.6	126.5	—	578.0
1976–1980	722.9	520.7	221.7	21.0	1.5	268.0	916.0
1981–1985	1,362.5	956.6	429.4	23.5	—	780.4	757.5
1986–1988	959.3	915.3	46.6	2.6	—	1,163.4	683.9
Total	3,291.1	2,430.7	774.7	42.5	128.0	2,211.8	2,935.4

*Wheat imports sold below cost.
Source: MAFF, *Major Statistics of Agriculture* (1989).

was an inherent limit on productivity. This meant that income parity between urban and farm households could be achieved only by increasing subsidies for agriculture. Although it is difficult to measure the exact net effect of the dual price system, it is generally believed that the system was important in narrowing the gap between urban and rural incomes in the 1970s. The dual price system for grain crops was an important policy measure for supporting rural income levels and achieving self-sufficiency in rice production. A side effect of these actions included a delay in the structural reorientation of the rural economy toward more competition and more diverse sources of income.

New Community Movement

As rural-urban disparity worsened in the 1960s, the government faced difficulties that it could no longer ignore. Increasing dependency on foreign food grains presented an economic problem by taking up large amounts of scarce foreign currency. Massive migration into large cities was a potential source of social instability. If the creation of the dual price system for rice and barley was a response to the economic problems of rural development, the New Community Movement (Saemaul Undong; hereafter, NCM) was more politically oriented. First introduced in a presidential address in 1970, full-scale NCM programs were launched in 1971.

The NCM was designed to improve life in rural villages by encouraging people to create, on their own, a better living environment and to raise their standard of living. With the guiding principles of hard work, self-reliance, cooperation, and a positive attitude toward self-improvement, the goal of the movement went beyond agricultural development. It tried to change the attitudes of the rural population as a whole, as well as raise rural living standards by improving rural infrastructure and amenities and by boosting production.

For individual households, the NCM improved toilet and sewage disposal systems, replaced thatched straw roofing with cement or ceramic tiles, modernized kitchen facilities, and repaired fences. Visible progress was made in improving the small-scale infrastructure in and around villages: community centers, laundry facilities, and public baths were constructed; water wells were repaired and streams embanked; farm feeder and village roads were improved. More ambitious villages installed electrical and telephone lines or constructed simple waterworks.

Improving living environments is an important goal, but living standards cannot be raised unless income grows. Measures taken to increase production included expansion of the production base (including extension of irrigation facilities, rural electrification, upgrading land fertility, and intensive utilization of arable land), cooperative farming practices (such as collective cultivation and harvesting, efforts to control pests and crop disease, and joint livestock and fish production), and the development of off-farm income sources (through reforestation projects and attraction of manufacturing factories to rural areas).

The Ministry of Home Affairs, with the entire administrative apparatus under its authority, was primarily responsible for guiding the movement, but other branches of the government were expected to give their full support.[22] At least in principle, villagers were chiefly responsible for finding resources and implementing projects, while the government provided only technical and financial assistance through subsidies and loans.

Government spending on the NCM is hard to estimate since even without the movement, rural electrification, expansion of communications networks, and other infrastructure projects would have taken place. Table 7-21 shows that the government's share of the NCM investment steadily increased, with the exception of 1981, when the nation was in political turmoil after the death of President Park. Spending stabilized at around 8 percent of the broadly defined welfare expenditure in the 1980s.

Table 7-21. Sources of Investment for New Community Movement Projects (billion *won*)

| | A | B | C | D | B/D |
	Total NCM Investment (B+C)	Government Subsidy	Private[a]	National Government Welfare Expenditure[b]	%
1971–1972	43.5	7.4	36.1	732.4	1.0
1973	98.4	21.5	76.9	432.8	5.0
1974	132.8	30.8	102.0	749.1	4.1
1975	295.9	165.3	130.6	1,065.5	15.5
1976	322.6	165.1	157.5	1,512.7	10.9
1977	466.5	246.0	220.5	1,969.2	12.5
1978	634.2	338.4	295.8	2,550.8	13.3
1979	758.2	425.2	333.0	3,845.1	11.1
1980	936.7	415.6	521.1	4,677.4	8.9
1981	702.9	419.4	283.5	6,433.8	6.5
1982	866.6	564.0	302.6	7,382.5	7.6
1983	987.0	625.0	362.0	7,560.8	8.3
1984	1,002.9	724.6	278.3	8,663.2	8.4
1985	1,040.7	761.8	278.9	9,508.4	8.0
1986	1,017.0	799.5	217.5	9,953.6	8.0
1987	1,168.7	1,001.4	167.3	11,933.2	8.4

[a]Paid by villagers in the form of labor, land, and cash.
[b]Total national government expenditure—Defense expenditure—general public service expenditure.
Sources: MHA, *Saemaul Movement* (1987); EPB, *Korea Statistical Yearbook* (1971-1987).

The experience of the NCM offers several valuable lessons. First, a viable grass-roots movement for self-improvement must start from the bottom, and the mere form of a democratic and voluntary organization is not enough to produce long-lasting results. Second, even if a true grass-roots organization is formed, continual financial and administrative support from the government is vital for its success. Finally, even if these two conditions are met, rural economic conditions cannot significantly improve without an understanding of the nature of rural-urban disparities and an appropriate strategy based on such knowledge. Although the NCM program did try to lure manufacturing establishments to rural regions, it did not address the serious problem of low productivity inherent in the structure of the agricultural sector.

Saemaul Factory Program
The Saemaul Factory program, which was designed to attract factories to rural areas, was a relatively minor part of the NCM. Given that farm income could not significantly improve within the existing agricultural structure and that off-farm income sources had to be developed, the goal of the program was important regardless of its scale or degree of success. It provided valuable lessons that aided the formation of rural industrialization programs in the 1980s.

The explicit objective of the program was to attract manufacturing establishments that would process locally produced raw materials and employ surplus labor in rural areas. It would provide rural areas with nonfarming income opportunities, simultaneously shifting manufacturing activities away from crowded cities. Initiated by a presidential order in 1973, the program's goal was to establish one Saemaul factory in each *Eup* (town) or *Myon* (village) by offering incentives in the form of tax reductions and loans.[23]

The program was not very successful in terms of the number of factories. In 1980, over 1,000 establishments were designated as Saemaul factories, and of these only 719 remained in operation at the end of the decade. Furthermore, compared to the composition of manufacturing nationally, the proportion of Saemaul factories in high-growth industries, such as metal and machinery production, was low (Table 7-22). In addition, only a few factories used local raw materials. Apparently most factories were lured into the program by low land prices, supposedly abundant labor, and government support.

By the end of 1986, according to a survey of Saemaul factories, for those factories operating under 80 percent of capacity, labor shortage was identified as the most serious bottleneck (see Table 7-23).[24] This fact

Table 7-22. Manufacturing Composition of Saemaul Factories, 1980

	Saemaul Factories (No.)	(%)	All Factories (No.)	(%)
Food and beverage	77	10.7	4,617	15.0
Textile, clothing and leather	245	34.1	7,682	24.9
Chemical and plastics	46	6.4	3,034	9.0
Metal, metal products, machinery, and equipment	99	13.8	7,532	24.4
Other	252	35.0	7,958	25.8

Sources: EPB, *Korea Statistical Yearbook* (1981); Jho Jung-Jay, "An Assessment of Korean Rural Industrialization Policies," *Korea Spatial Planning Review* 10 (September 1988).

has an important implication. Although rural areas supplied much labor to urban-industrial development, any attempt at rural industrialization required a certain concentration of population, or at least the prospect of it. The Saemaul Factory program was overly ambitious in trying to establish one factory in each basic administrative unit (*Eup* and *Myon*), since those units offered little in terms of banking, marketing, information processing, and other services, or an abundant supply of labor. For a rural industrialization program to be successful, it must recognize that the target area must meet certain necessary preconditions of a suitable business environment. Since these conditions could hardly be met in remote *Eup* and *Myon* areas, the basic planning unit had to be larger than these units. This lesson was taken into account in the next industrialization policy, the rural industrial estate (RIE) development program.

Table 7-23. Reasons for Under-Capacity Operation of Saemaul Factories (%)

Factories in Operation, but under 80 Percent of Capacity[a]		Factories Not in Operation[b]	
Raw material supply	26.8	Finance	71.1
Labor supply	33.9	Sales	14.5
Sales	14.3	Raw material	7.2
Finance	8.9	Under refurbishing	7.2
Others	16.1		

[a] Total of 56 out of 197 factories surveyed were found to be operating under 80 percent of capacity.
[b] Eighty-three factories were not in operation in December 1985.
Sources: Jho, "An Assessment"; Kim Jong-Gie and Il-Chung Hwang, *Characteristics of Rural Industries and Policies for Rural Industrialization* (Seoul: Korea Development Institute, 1987), reproduced with permission.

Rural Development and Agricultural Policies in the 1980s

Researchers and policymakers gradually formed a consensus that for rural income to sustain continued growth, two mutually complementary policy directions needed to be followed. First, the structure of agriculture had to change in accordance with forces both internal and external to the sector. Second, to raise living standards, sources of off-farm income had to expand, supplementing agricultural income. According to Table 7-24, the proportion of off-farm income in total farm household income gradually increased from 24 percent in 1970 to 40 percent in 1988.

Structural Adjustment of Agriculture

The basic idea behind the call for structural adjustment in the agricultural sector was that agricultural income could not continue to rise without a corresponding increase in productivity. The dual price system already was a burden to the national economy, but even if the government maintained the level of support for the dual price system, the productivity gap between the manufacturing and agricultural sectors had widened. The most important factor restricting increases in agricultural productivity was the small scale of farming units established by land reform policy. The Land Reform Act put an upper limit (approximately 3 hectares) on the amount of farmland a household could own. It also impeded free transactions to combine farm plots since the sale of all farmland had to be approved by the local government.

Table 7-24. Composition of Farm Household Income (percentages)

	Agricultural Income	Total Off-Farm Income	Off-Farm Income Side Business Salaries	Wages and Donations	Wealth and Assets
1962	79.6	20.4	3.8	9.4	7.2
1965	79.2	20.8	3.5	8.9	8.4
1970	75.9	24.1	3.8	10.4	9.9
1975	81.9	18.1	2.5	9.4	6.2
1977	72.3	27.7	2.7	12.5	12.5
1980	65.2	34.8	2.5	14.5	17.8
1983	65.0	35.0	3.6	13.0	18.4
1985	64.5	35.5	3.7	13.8	18.0
1987	61.5	38.5	4.3	14.6	19.6
1988	60.4	39.6	4.3	17.5	17.8

Sources: MAFF, *Major Statistics of A.F.F.* (1989); Kim Jong-Gie, *Rural Industrialization in Korea*, KDI Working Paper (September 1983).

Table 7-25. Farm Size Distribution

	Average Farm Size per Household (hectares)	Farm Size Distribution (percentage)				
		Under 0.1 hectare	Under 0.5 hectare	Under 1 hectare	Under 3 hectare	Over 3 hectare
1965	0.90	2.8	33.1	31.7	31.2	1.2
1970	0.93	1.1	31.6	34.2	31.6	1.5
1975	0.94	0.1	30.2	36.2	31.9	1.6
1980	1.02	0.7	28.1	35.2	34.6	1.5
1985	1.11	0.5	27.9	36.5	33.9	1.2
1988	1.17	0.4	27.8	34.9	35.4	1.4

Note: Farm size means area of cultivated land. A hectare is equal to 10,000 square meters, or 2.47 acres.
Source: MAFF, *Major Statistics of A.F.F.* (1989).

Restrictions on farm size limited agricultural productivity by preventing farms from taking advantage of economies-of-scale associated with large farms. The small scale limited the output of each farm and raised production costs by restricting the use of labor-saving machinery. For example, it has been estimated that even with a 40 percent subsidy for farm machinery purchases, the breakeven farm size was 2.9 hectares for a rice transplanter, 4.5 hectares for a combine, and 9.5 hectares for a tractor.[25] Farmers could not take advantage of this labor-saving technology unless farm sizes increased. Although farms gradually increased in size as small, unsustainable farms closed down and population in the agricultural sector decreased (Table 7-25), this small increase was not enough to close the productivity gap between agriculture and industry.[26]

Rural Industrial Estate Program

As the Saemaul Factory program stagnated, the direction of rural industrialization policy shifted. The RIE program began in 1984. Instead of establishing a manufacturing enterprise in each remote area, as attempted by the factory program, the new strategy called for the development of industrial estates in rural population centers that could provide viable business environments. Rural manufacturing factories would be concentrated in these estates and employ workers from the vicinity, who would commute to work.

RIE incentives offered greater benefits to individual firms than those given under the Saemaul Factory program and thus better compensated firms that moved to the rural areas. The number of industrial parks and factories established in rural areas rose fast (Table 7-26), and many of

Table 7-26. Rural Industrial Estate Designation

	Number of RIEs	Area (1,000 *pyong*)[a]	Number of Factories Planned
Trends			
1985	7	184	78
1986	24	706	232
1987	46	2,248	490
1988	45	2,010	555
1989	45	2,352	445
Total	167	7,500	1,800
Distribution among provinces (as of 1987)			
Kyonggi	1	33	8
Kangwon	5	205	57
North Ch'ungch'ong	18	621	141
South Ch'ungch'ong	19	690	235
North Cholla	7	290	38
South Cholla	8	548	95
North Kyongsang	10	305	93
South Kyongsang	9	273	76
Total	77	2,966	743

[a]1 *pyong* = 3.3m^2.
Note: The discrepancy between tables is due to differences in original sources.
Sources: MAFF, *Major Statistics of A.F.F.* (1989); MCT, *Industrial Estates* (1988).

them were concentrated in high-growth industries such as metal products, machinery, and equipment.

An enthusiastic response from the private sector as well as from local governments suggested that the RIE's strategy had been successful, at least in comparison with the Saemaul Factory program, and that business environments in rural areas improved enough to allow manufacturing bases to be created. Four factors had positive effects on the RIE program. First, RIEs were developed in small cities with populations of fewer than 200,000 or in rural population centers. These bases began to grow rapidly after the early 1980s, providing the necessary labor force for manufacturing activities. Second, rural infrastructure, especially roads and communication facilities, improved significantly. Firms located in the RIEs no longer suffered from the bottlenecks experienced by the Saemaul factories. Third, for an individual firm, the remaining locational disadvantages could be offset by a broad range of incentives. Since high land prices and strict regulations on land use made it almost impossible for small and medium-sized firms to find factory sites in large cities, RIEs were one of the few alternatives for relocation or establishment of second factories. Fourth, local governments were given discretionary power in planning and developing RIEs, as well as in allocating financial and administrative assistance from the central government. Having learned from the NCM experience, local governments became more responsive to local development. The sale of factory sites provided large windfall gains to supplement their budgets. Local governments appeared more qualified than any central planning agency to make judgments about the location, size, and nature of RIEs, and about which firms best matched local conditions.

The RIE program nevertheless did have some problems. First, RIEs were developed to meet the needs of city manufacturing firms. They were often located in South and North Chungchong provinces, too close to Seoul. Second, unskilled workers did not always receive the benefits of employment and higher income, especially when factories moved only to take advantage of the cheap land and government incentives, and set up automated production lines. Third, since agriculture has a large seasonal variation in labor requirements, some RIEs had difficulty maintaining a steady labor supply, which is necessary for smooth operation and training. Fourth, incentives given to RIE factories put some firms outside the estates at a competitive disadvantage. Despite these problems, the RIE program learned from the failures of the past and served as the basic framework for rural industrialization in the 1990s.

Conclusion

Rural out-migration has been the most prominent interregional population trend in Korea. The disparity between rural and urban areas was perceived as a serious problem by the Korean government, and policies directed toward resolving the problem were required by political realities, if not on grounds of equity or efficiency. Over the long course of rural decline, the government made frequent attempts at intervention, but an effective strategy has been formulated slowly, and after much trial and error.

Entering the 1990s, rural Korea faced new challenges and opportunities, among them international pressure to open markets for agricultural products, large debts inherited from the 1980s, and the introduction of local autonomy. One prediction is that increased investment and coordinated efforts by the government will be necessary to keep rural-urban disparities from widening.

NOTES

1. For a more comprehensive description of changes in the settlement system of Korea, see Hwang Myong-Chan and Jin-Ho Choi, "Evolution

of the Settlement System in Korea: A Historical Perspective," in Hwang Myong-Chan and Harry W. Richardson, eds., *Urban and Regional Policy in Korea and International Experiences* (Seoul: Kon-Kuk University Press, 1986).

2. Between 1966 and 1970, the average annual rate of population growth in Seoul was a remarkable 9.8 percent. The population of Tokyo grew at an annual rate of 5.3 percent between 1950 and 1955. In most developing countries between 1950 and 1975, the rate of urbanization averaged 2 to 3 percent; in Korea the rate was much faster, at 4.1 percent.

3. Official publication of the data stopped after 1978.

4. World Bank, *Korea: Spatial Strategy Review* (Washington, D.C.: World Bank, 1986).

5. In addition, each agency has often changed sampling units, survey methods, and range of gross income and costs. Such changes frequently biased the statistics in favor of rural households.

6. See Ban Sung-Hwan, Pal-Yong Moon, and Dwight Perkins, *Rural Development* (Cambridge: Council on East Asian Studies, Harvard University, 1980).

7. Choo Hak-Chung and J. Yoon, "Size Distribution of Income in Korea, 1982: Its Estimation and Sources of Changes," *Korea Development Review* (1984), (in Korean).

8. Choo Hak-Chung, *Widening Urban-Rural Income Differentials in Korea: A Reexamination,* KDI Working Paper 8205, (August 1982), p. 12.

9. Ibid.

10. This classification is not clear-cut. For instance, tapwater, roads, electricity, telephone, and other servces are important for both consumption and production.

11. Kim Jong-Gie, "The Effect of Infrastructure Investment on Regional Development in Korea, 1970–1985," *Korea Development Review* 9, no. 3 (1987) (in Korean), studied regional disparity of infrastructural provision among provinces for the period 1970 to 1985. For most categories, the disparity significantly decreased.

12. Urban housing units had more floor space than their rural counterparts, but there were more households residing in urban housing units.

13. Among *Kun* residents, the three greatest inconveniences cited in 1987 were those related to medical services (46.4 percent), shopping (21.4 percent), and civil services (13.6 percent). Among *Shi* residents, they were related to shopping (36.9 percent), medical services (21.6 percent), and lack of open space (14.3 percent). Economic Planning Board, *Social Indicators in Korea* (1988).

14. Regional policies usually lack indisputable theoretical justification. Equity is frequently cited, but Hong Sung-Woong, "Balancing Equity and Efficiency in Regional Policy," in Hwang and Richardson, *Urban and Regional Policy,* argues that helping poor regions does not necessarily help poor people. We do not attempt to establish a theoretical basis for regional policies but simply recognize the pressures imposed on policymakers.

15. The responsibility for balanced regional development shifted among ministries so often (five times between 1969 and 1981) that we cannot but feel that it was a political hot potato.

16. For more details about the National Physical Development Plans, see Lee Jeong-Sik, "Regional Development Policies in Korea, Retrospective and Prospects," *Korea Spatial Planning Review* (September 1988), and Kwon Won-Yong, "Regional Development Policies and Strategies for the Sixth Economic and Social Development Plan (1987–1991)," in Hwang and Richardson, *Urban and Regional Policy.*

17. The World Bank Report (*Korea: Spatial Strategy Review*) argued that suburbanization beyond the green belt was a wasteful use of land considering the long daily trip of commuters and commodities.

18. Kangnung at best was a medium-sized city (population of 144,000 in 1987), but it was the center of the mountainous northeast coastal region.

19. Kwon, "Regional Development Policies."

20. In this period, the dual price system has a very different meaning from the later period. Before 1960 the government purchase price was below production cost, and the government forced farmers to sell their crops at a low price by prohibiting free disposal. In the 1960s, the purchase price rose above the production cost, but it still was below the market price.

21. In 1972, the fund's borrowing from the central bank amounted to 13.3 percent of the total increase in money supply. The ratio went up to 98.2 percent in 1975. Moon Pal-Yong et al., *Rural Development in Korea* (Seoul: Korea Development Institute, 1981), p. 220 (in Korean).

22. The NCM may have had a positive effect in changing the attitudes of local government officials. They were traditionally instruments of enforcing order, conscription, election management, and taxation. The NCM forced them to pay attention to rural development projects that could not be successfully accomplished without the cooperation of residents. However, central management of the movement along local administrative lines had its problems. See Moon Pal-Yong et al., *Rural Development in Korea* (Seoul: Korea Development Institute, 1981), pp. 236–241 (in Korean).

23. In 1970, there were 91 *Eup* and 1,376 *Myon*. The figures in 1989 were 179 and 1,260.

24. In Table 7-23 the reasons for under-capacity operation and shut-down are quite different, especially in the ratio of firms giving "finance" as a reason. This is probably due to "finance" being an ambiguous term that may include many different kinds of managerial difficulties. Also, it is unfortunate that "labor shortage" was not included as a possible answer in the second survey.

25. Song Dae-Hee and Byong-Suh Yoo, *Structural Adjustment of Agriculture in the Age of Industrialization* (Seoul: Korea Development Institute, 1985) (in Korean).

26. A 1985 Korea Development Institute report on agriculture encouraged the creation of large farms and proposed that the landownership limit be raised to 10 hectares, that the partition of farmland by inheritance be discouraged, and that farmland leasing be legalized. Ibid., pp. 126–131.

8

Conclusion: The Strains of Economic Growth

David L. Lindauer

The advantage of economic growth is not that wealth increases happiness, but that it increases the range of human choice. It is very hard to correlate wealth and happiness. Happiness results from the way one looks at life, taking it as it comes, dwelling on the pleasant rather than the unpleasant, and living without fear of what the future may bring. Wealth would increase happiness if it increased resources more than it increased wants, but it does not necessarily do this, and there is no evidence that the rich are happier than the poor, or that individuals grow happier as their incomes increase.
—Arthur Lewis

Armed with the knowledge of what Korea has achieved, imagine going back in time and returning to Korea in the early 1960s. Imagine encountering a typical Korean production worker of that era and telling him about his country's and, in some sense, his own economic future. We say that from the mid-1960s well into the 1980s, there will be an explosion of employment growth. New jobs in manufacturing will increase at a rate of roughly 8 percent per annum, yielding an almost fivefold increase in the employment of production workers. Not only will job opportunities expand swiftly, but wages will grow equally fast. And although price inflation at times will be a problem, the purchasing power of these wages will double, on average, every nine years.

Next imagine encountering a Korean farmer of the early 1960s. We tell him that his sons and daughters will be leaving the countryside, as will many of his neighbors and their children. Many farm communities will be depopulated by the end of the 1980s as Korea rapidly becomes urbanized. Seoul alone will have a population in excess of 10 million people, accounting for one of every four South Koreans. Although many of our farmer's friends and family will depart for cities, the rural economy will not be left behind. The gap between rural and urban household income will rise and fall, but by the end of two decades, rural households will boast income gains that rival those of urban production workers.

Hearing this news, our early 1960s production worker and farmer, surveying the poverty around them, can only conclude that our vision of Korea's economic future is nothing less than a miracle. Yet what would they say if we add that by 1990, despite these remarkable material gains, a large percentage of Korean workers and farmers would be dissatisfied with their economic circumstances. "How can this be?" reply our production worker and farmer. "No, you must be mistaken. Only a group of radicals or dissidents could be dissatisfied if what you have told us is true."

The reasons for considering the contradiction between Korea's economic record and discontent over economic outcomes are straight-forward. Within Korea, insight into the determinants of dissatisfaction with economic outcomes might contribute to a better understanding of past events and could offer suggestions for forging an improved social contract. Outside of Korea, greater appreciation of the strains that have accompanied Korea's drive toward economic maturity may point the way toward reducing such strains in those low- and middle-income countries that hope to follow Korea's path.

Findings reported by the authors of this book support the view that discontent over economic outcomes in Korea was widespread by the late 1980s. Survey results on individual satisfaction with social and economic conditions reported by Lim (Chapter 1) indicate that close to half of the respondents maintained a perception of "absolute or relative deprivation" (Tables 2-11 and 2-12). Lee and Lindauer (Chapter 5) evaluate the degree of job dissatisfaction reported by Korean labor and find levels of dissatisfaction over wages and working conditions approaching 50 percent for production and service workers (Table 5-6). The qualitative approach employed by Vogel and Lindauer (Chapter 6) concludes that Korea's unprecedented wave of labor unrest that began in 1987 should be understood in terms of long-held grievances by workers over pecu-niary and nonpecuniary issues. Kim and Son (Chapter 7) call attention to regional disparities and ensuing tensions, as well as to the distrust by farmers of the government's commitment to the rural economy. Taken together, the evidence suggests that in spite of (or maybe because of) the nation's economic miracle, many Koreans reported themselves dissatisfied with their personal economic situation.

In searching for explanations of popular discontent, we begin with some political hypotheses. Were our 1960s production worker and farmer correct? Were radicals ultimately behind the expression of dissatisfaction with economic outcomes in the late 1980s? This viewpoint is held not only by our two imaginary Koreans, but was shared by many Korean citizens, including those in positions of power in government and business. In their view, radicals, particularly the *uijang* or students disguised as workers, infiltrated the labor movement and sowed the seeds of discontent. Vogel and Lindauer reject this interpretation, arguing that the *uijang* at most served as catalysts. Given the widespread nature of social unrest, it must have had deeper roots than the rhetoric and organizational skills of the *uijang*.

A more persuasive political hypothesis links discontent over economic outcomes with the pent-up frustration over authoritarian rule. It is no coincidence that strike activity exploded in 1987, the same year that Korea's move toward democratization began. In a newly liberalized political environment and with few political institutions to choose from, labor disturbances (as well as student protests) may have presented the best opportunities for displaying dissatisfaction with the nation's legacy of political repression. To the extent that labor unrest served as an expression of political opposition, strike activity cannot be viewed solely as an indicator of worker economic discontent.

The Economics of Discontent

Legitimate Economic Grievances

Although political factors played a role, the chapters in this book argue that the dissatisfaction of specific groups in the economy was based, at least in part, on legitimate economic grievances.

The rapid transformation of rural labor into a modern, industrial workforce, coupled with the overall growth in real earnings and employment, suggests that Korean labor was a partner in the nation's economic growth. These results are especially impressive when compared to the experience of labor in other successful middle-income economies (Chapter 3). In terms of the growth in real earnings, the expansion of productive employment, and labor's claim on value-added, Korean workers in manufacturing did better than their counterparts in any of the other "success" cases.

But the average Korean compares himself not to a Brazilian, Turkish, or even Japanese worker but to those within his own economy, and Korean labor maintains that others—most notably large business owners—did far better. Official data, as well as the consensus position of previous studies, indicate that the distribution of income in Korea started from a base of relative equality at the end of the Korean War, became even more equal during the 1960s, witnessed rising inequality in the 1970s, and returned to growing equality during the 1980s. The distribution of wealth appears to have followed a different path. The growing concentration of Korea's industrial structure—the result, in part, of the rapid expansion of many privately held *chaebol*—and the increased inequality of assets, especially land, significantly skewed Korea's wealth distribution in the 1980s.[1] When these trends are taken into consideration, the position that Korea's working class experienced some relative deterioration in their standard of living during the 1980s is sustained. Whether such deterioration represents a legitimate economic grievance is considered later.

When evaluating trends in the distribution of wage income alone, we find considerable evidence of increasing equality of relative pay across Korean workers (Chapter 4). This finding takes on added significance in the light of the tremendous expansion of employment in the wage sector between 1965 and 1986. Not only did workers move toward a more equal sharing of labor income, but labor income proceeded to represent larger percentages of total income. When combined, these tendencies exerted a significant influence on improving the overall distribution of household income.

The results on improving wage equality appear robust when account is taken of the trends in the nonagricultural, small-scale sector of the economy. Although the data are limited, the results on manufacturing support the findings of more casual observations. The proliferation of small-scale enterprises did not suggest a growing economic underclass of low-productivity jobs and underemployed workers. Instead, small enterprises offered remunerative and competitive employment opportunities. The narrowing of the wage gap between small and large firms implies that the overwhelming number of workers employed in small enterprises were not left behind as the economy moved toward greater industrial sophistication.

The increasing equality of wages is a statement about trends but not about levels. And it is the level of wage inequality, even after a decade of narrowing, that differentiates Korea's wage structure from that of other economies and may have contributed to the dissatisfaction we are trying to understand. High premiums accrued to Korea's men, educated workers, and white-collar occupations. It also appears that returns to human capital investments, including schooling, disproportionately accrued to white-collar, especially managerial, occupations. All of Korea's workforce became more experienced and educated, but the benefits of this training were considerably greater for managers than for production workers. Increased schooling and experience raised labor's aspirations, but relative wage rewards did not keep pace, contributing, perhaps, to the widespread tension between blue- and white-collar workers.

Regarding another unequal dimension of Korea's wage structure, there is little evidence that male-female pay differences generated a response similar to the tension over occupational differentials. Calls for equal pay for men and women, wages based on comparable worth, or affirmative action for Korean women in hiring were not part of labor's agenda as they were in most of the more advanced industrial nations. Why the wide and persistent wage gap between Korean men and women did not appear to contribute to labor's dissatisfaction may be explained by both economic and cultural factors. Traditional attitudes (held by men and women alike) about women's role in the labor market were maintained in Korea, even as female labor force participation grew to the point where women accounted for close to half of all production jobs. Women generally had short attachments to the labor force, and their earnings were not expected to play a significant role in supporting household income. Furthermore, female-headed households, a growing social group in the United States with primary economic responsibility for their families, were a minuscule proportion of Korean households.

Along some margin, Korea's unequal wage structure contributed to the perception of relative deprivation voiced by many workers. Why Korea continued to have a relatively unequal pay structure remains unclear. The role of custom, as Park and Park (1984) contend, is one element.[2] Amsden argues that the needs and practices of Korea's diversified business groups, the *chaebol*, provide another answer. She suggests that the labor skills required of late industrializers include a workforce willing and able to learn new production processes. An implicit contract is struck with workers, and in return for higher wages, workers provide greater effort and loyalty. There is merit to Amsden's efficiency wage explanation, especially for managerial and supervisory positions. High turnover rates, however, cast doubt on the applicability of Amsden's wage-loyalty nexus for explaining interindustry pay differentials among production workers. In addition, Korea's high level of earnings dispersion, evident from at least the early 1970s and continuing through the present, predates the emergence of the *chaebol* as dominant economic agents in the labor market. Other explanations are still needed to determine why (and when) a "labor aristocracy" in Korea emerged.[3]

Worker dissatisfaction can also be tied to the nonpecuniary character of working life. There is considerable truth to the gloomy portrait of workers in Korea in the 1980s facing the world's longest workweek and exposed to unsafe working conditions (Chapter 5). The average officially reported workweek in manufacturing of fifty-two to fifty-six hours exceeded the hours reported by any other nation. Meanwhile, industrial accidents, including fatalities, increased as the mix of industrial activity, including growth in construction and shipbuilding, became riskier. Although the frequency of injury and fatalities declined, international data on industrial safety (admittedly of questionable accuracy) give no indication that Korea's record on job safety was an enviable one.

Long hours and hazardous workplaces were symptomatic of one of Korean labor's deepest grievances: the poor treatment workers received from their employers. In contrast to Japanese businesses' pride in the paternalism of their enterprises and the alleged harmony of interest among employees, Korean labor's refrain all too often was, "We want to be treated like human beings!" Labor's dissatisfaction with their working lives was in response to the militaristic discipline of the shop floor and the systematic repression of labor's independent voice (Chapter 6). With rising levels of per capita income, traditional systems of labor management and control were no longer tolerable, especially to younger Korean workers. Although real wages rose dramatically, the increase was insufficient to compensate labor for the treatment they received or the independent representation labor desired but had long been deprived of.

Rural households also expressed dissatisfaction with economic policies and outcomes. Although measures of income disparity show that the gap between rural and urban areas narrowed considerably after the 1960s, other measures tell a different story (Chapter 7). Since most industrial estates were planned and supported by the government, manufacturing industries and their attendant linkages were concentrated along the Seoul-Pusan axis. Broad measures of social and economic infrastructure suggested a similar trend. Economic infrastructure, including paved roads, telephone, and water and sewerage services, was vital for attracting investment capital and the subsequent generation of employment and growth of regional incomes. The spatial development of this infrastructure revealed that the gap between city and countryside was large and had widened over time. Social infrastructure, such as housing and educational, medical, and cultural facilities, offered further evidence of this widening gap.

When evaluating relative deprivation along geographic lines, it is important to remember that relatively easy internal migration offered a critical and in many ways effective mechanism for responding to regional imbalances. Many of those rural households, or residents of relatively neglected provinces like the Chollas, who might otherwise have suffered the direct consequences of regional economic inequality, moved to more prosperous cities. Migration mitigated the problems associated with the pattern of Korea's spatial development, but with close to one out of every four Koreans living in rural areas as of 1990, regional imbalances and inequities remained significant economic and political issues.

Expectations and Perceptions

Whether the economic grievances just summarized were in some absolute sense legitimate, many Koreans believed they were. Expectations about economic rewards are an integral part of the explanation for why Korean workers and other social groups felt such discontent over economic outcomes. If expectations grow faster than resources, dissatisfaction can be anticipated even if the rate of economic progress is rapid. Since problems associated with rising expectations long have been recognized, here we consider whether there are any circumstances specific to Korea that have widened the gap between expectations and outcomes.[4]

One possibility is that rapid growth itself contributed to heightened expectations. Even if relative incomes remained roughly the same, rapid as opposed to more moderate growth quickly expanded the absolute income gap between households. It is this expanding absolute income gap that ultimately supported the consumption of significantly different goods between upper-, middle-, and lower-income families. At low levels of per capita income, the goods that households of different income levels consume may be relatively similar. Higher-income families may consume more of certain goods, but food and other necessities still command a high percentage of disposable income. By comparison, once per capita income levels reach a certain point, the consumption bundle of well-to-do households—including automobiles, imported clothing, and other forms of conspicuous consumption—becomes quite distinct from the goods and services consumed by middle- and lower-income groups. Since rapid growth can bring about these visible changes in consumption patterns in a relatively short period of time, rapid growth itself may have contributed to the rising—and frustrated—expectations of the majority.

If rapid growth per se was a source of economic discontent, we would expect to observe popular dissatisfaction with economic outcomes not only in Korea but in other rapidly growing economies. Taiwan experienced popular discontent in the 1980s similar to what occurred in Korea, but Taiwanese protests may have been based even more on political considerations than was the case in Korea. Japanese experience is more revealing. By the end of Japan's period of rapid growth,

1950–1973, one finds a distinct similarity between the language used by Japanese and Koreans to describe their respective situations. The frequent and pejorative reference to Japan's industrial strategy of "production first"[5] is analogous to the 1980s' Korean criticism of the nation's "growth-first strategy." In both settings the implication is that rapid growth may have benefited "someone else, but not me." In describing social attitudes toward economic achievements in Japan in the late 1960s, Bennett and Levine, in a study of postindustrial society in Japan entitled, "Industrialization and Social Deprivation," note, "Despite the impressive gains after the mid 1950s, by the late 1960s the growing disparity between economic growth and social welfare had gained wide recognition by both liberal and conservative elements of Japanese society."[6]

Feelings of relative deprivation emerged and were widely articulated following a period of rapid growth in both Korea and Japan. Dissatisfaction with the fruits of rapid growth in these countries exhibits similarities, but there are important differences as well, in terms of both the form of protest and the locus of dissatisfaction. More attention in Japan was focused on environmental issues and failures in the provision of public goods. Issues of distribution took on more importance in Korea.

Popular discontent over economic outcomes in Korea also seemed tied to perceptions and reactions to income inequality itself, that is, independent of the rate of economic growth. As stated in this book and elsewhere, the distribution of income in Korea appeared quite equal by international standards, even after acknowledging some deterioration from the late l960s. Korea's low rural-urban income gap, the small urban underclass of underemployed labor, and the rapid expansion of wage employment in the modern economy all contributed to this progressive distributional outcome.

Why, then, is there apparently so little tolerance in Korea for income differences that would be considered modest in most other economies? To understand Korean sensitivities toward income inequality, recall that as recently as the early 1960s, Korea was essentially a classless and homogeneous society. The reasons for this equality in poverty are well known: a half-century of exploitative colonial rule, a post–Pacific War redistributive land reform, and a cataclysmic civil war that destroyed whatever meager assets households had accumulated. Because of both its racial homogeneity and unique historical experience, Korea began its growth miracle with greater equality than can be observed in almost any other twentieth-century development experience.

With Korea's historical legacy of income equality, is it surprising that the inherent unevenness of the development process would breed more resentment than occurs elsewhere? Furthermore, many Koreans believe the achievements of the majority of the well-to-do were tainted since they were due less to personal sacrifice and talents than to government favors and unfair advantages. Popular expressions of relative deprivation may have reflected indignation toward economic favoritism as much as any real or economic hardship. This is not meant to suggest that such intolerance is unjustified, but rather that, given the historic basis of Korean attitudes toward inequality, Koreans may articulate economic grievances that would not be as much of an issue in other settings. Economic grievances were more likely to arise in Korea than in other nations because the historical precedent of income equality continued to play a significant role in shaping individual expectations about the distribution of economic gains.

Lessons

In the 1990s, labor unrest and other forms of social protest subsided in Korea. Does this imply that earlier grievances either had been resolved or forgotten? Probably not. Most social movements experience an ebb and flow, and the current period of relative calm in Korea should be taken advantage of to reflect on the nation's experience.

Koreans first should recognize and acknowledge the incredible achievements of their economy. Unless all the data are wrong or somehow have been engineered, the overwhelming evidence is that the average Korean household made remarkable material progress. Given that economic growth, wherever it occurs, is inherently an uneven and unbalanced process, Korea's ability to distribute its growth widely is a remarkable achievement that few other societies can claim.

But it should also be recognized that Korea's economic miracle has been flawed. Restricting criticism only to economic matters, there are legitimate grievances related to both distributional outcomes and the quality of working life. It is the conclusion of many of the authors of this book that the source of some of these flaws can be identified. A reliance on market forces coupled with an unwillingness to use government intervention to correct for specific market failures generated economic outcomes that helped to spawn popular dissatisfaction. Competitive forces were an essential element in generating employment, raising wages, and narrowing the variance in the earnings structure. Competition was critical to permitting the vast small-scale sector of the economy to keep pace with large enterprises and not to devolve into a repository of unproductive and underemployed labor. Market forces similarly were vital in enabling migration to counter the unevenness of regional growth and reduce the hardships more commonly associated with differential spatial development.

But market forces cannot be relied on or expected to generate all the improvements associated with economic development. In situations where collective action rather than the atomistic workings of the market is pivotal, the state has an obligation to intervene and promote due process. Redistribution, along class, gender, or geographic lines, at times requires explicit interventions, especially when sensitivities toward social equity are heightened.

Do these arguments imply that over the past decades the Korean government should have intervened to redistribute income between labor and capital, reduce the workweek, and support the formation of an independent trade union movement? These questions cannot be answered without explicitly considering the trade-offs implicit in such actions. To what extent would a lower rate of growth in gross national product have resulted, and would the trade-off have been welfare-improving?

Counterfactuals such as these are not easily answered, although arguments presented in this book suggest that growth need not always be sacrificed for the attainment of other economic and social objectives. In some situations, where growth must be sacrificed for improvements in the quality of national development, the trade-off may be worth making. By considering those areas that ignited popular protest, we call attention to the areas that government should consider as appropriate and promising for progressive interventions.

As other low- and middle-income nations look to Korea for direction and inspiration, they should dwell not on the strains but on the requirements for rapid economic growth. Recognition and anticipation of the strains that accompany growth may permit those countries that follow Korea to lessen the unrest and dissatisfaction that Korea witnessed. A development strategy that rapidly increases material rewards while simultaneously reducing these strains would truly be miraculous.

NOTES

1. For a summary of previous work see Danny M. Leipziger et al., *The Distribution of Income and Wealth in Korea*, EDI Development Studies (Washington, D.C.: World Bank, 1992).

2. Fun-Koo Park and Se-Il Park, *Wage Structure in Korea* (Seoul: Korea Development Institute, 1984).

3. Alice Amsden, "South Korea's Record Wage Rates: Labor in Late Industrialization," *Industrial Relations* 29, no. 1 (Winter 1990), views the Korean labor market as one of segmented markets. The intertemporal movement in Korea's earnings structure, however, seems more consistent with competitive forces than with market segmentation. But Gary S. Fields, "Industrialization and Employment in Hong Kong, Korea, Singapore, and Taiwan," in Walter Galenson, ed., *Foreign Trade and Investment: Economic Growth in the Newly Industrializing Asian Countries* (Madison: University of Wisconsin Press, 1985) contends that wage and employment outcomes in Korea are purely competitive and market determined, a conclusion that seems to deny the wide and unexplained dispersion in earnings. A hybrid of these two positions is likely to be most accurate. Competitive forces are powerful in Korea's labor market, but they operate within a wage system that maintains a number of institutional rigidities.

4. James C. Davies, "Toward a Theory of Revolution," *American Sociological Review* 27 (February 1962), presents the so-called J-curve explanation for social revolutions, a well known social-psychological theory based on rising expectations. Such expectations may be formed during a period of economic progress. According to Davies' theory, a sudden economic downturn can foment social revolution as these expectations become frustrated.

5. John W. Bennett and Solomon B. Levine, "Industrialization and Social Deprivation: Welfare, Environment, and the Postindustrial Society in Japan," in Hugh Patrick, ed., *Japanese Industrialization and Its Social Consequences* (Berkeley: University of California Press, 1976), p. 442.

6. Ibid., p. 448.

9

Epilogue: Labor Outcomes in the 1990s

David L. Lindauer

By 1990, strike activity in Korea had subsided dramatically. Three years earlier, in 1987, there had been 3,617 officially recorded labor disputes; in 1990 there were only 322. There are several explanations for this turnaround. First, labor had won many of its battles and ended the decade having recorded spectacular increases in real wages. Labor also had won the right to represent itself before management; it had found its voice. Second, starting in 1990, government took a harder line against union activity and resumed some of its anti-labor practices. Third, after three years of almost constant activity, much of it militant, the labor movement might have been worn out. Among average workers, the rapid democratization of the society, as it moved toward electing its first president without ties to the military, may have overwhelmed attention to labor issues.

The decline in strike activity continued well into the decade (Table 9-1). By 1995, only eighty-eight labor disputes were recorded. Such a low level had last been recorded in 1982. But there was one key difference. In 1982, eighty-eight strikes resulted in the loss of only 11,000 working days. In 1995, eighty-eight strikes caused almost 400,000 lost working days. In the earlier and repressive period, strikes were more likely to be wildcat strikes, less organized, limited to smaller establishments, and crushed quickly. After 1987, strikes were more prevalent among Korea's largest firms, were well organized, and could last for weeks or even months.

The decline in labor unrest is further captured by the exception to the rule. In the summer of 1993, Hyundai faced a two-month strike involving Hyundai Motor Company and other group members. Sixty thousand workers struck. The government called for riot troops to end the strike, and the eventual settlement netted Hyundai workers far less than they had demanded. Even more significant, this outbreak of labor unrest did not spawn an Ulsan Typhoon. It was limited to the Hyundai

Table 9-1. Labor Disputes, 1980–1994

Year	Number of Strikes	Working Days Lost (in thousands)
1980	206	61
1981	186	31
1982	88	11
1983	98	7
1984	114	20
1985	265	64
1986	276	72
1987	3,617	6,947
1988	1,873	5,401
1989	1,616	6,351
1990	322	4,487
1991	234	3,271
1992	235	1,528
1993	144	1,308
1994	121	1,484
1995	88	393

Sources: Ministry of Labor, *Yearbook of Labor Statistics* (various years); OECD, *OECD Economic Surveys: Korea* (1996).

group, where contentious labor-management relations had been the rule both before and after the events of the late 1980s.

In many ways labor outcomes and labor relations in the 1990s were reminiscent of the years prior to 1987. With the benefit of a few more years of hindsight, it seems appropriate to consider whether the late 1980s were an aberration or ushered in fundamental change.

The late 1980s were unique in terms of both labor unrest and real wage growth. During the twenty years 1966 to 1986, real wages in manufacturing annually grew by 7.7 percent. From 1986 to 1990, under the constant pressure of labor activity, they increased, on average, 12.2 percent per year. From 1990 to 1994 that average would return to 7.5 percent.

One of the legacies of the period of increased labor activity was a fall in working hours. In 1986, according to Ministry of Labor data, average hours in manufacturing stood at 54.2 per week. By 1990 they had declined to 49.8 and by 1994 stood at 48.7, a 10 percent drop over these eight years. Starting in 1993, Korea could no longer claim the world's longest workweek in manufacturing; Singapore held this dubious distinction.

Industrial fatalities did not follow a similar trajectory. In 1994, 2,678 fatalities were reported, a record level exceeding the number reported in 1986 by over 1,000. Although the injury rate continued to decline and more accurate reporting probably contributed to the measured increase in fatalities, the hazardous nature of work in Korea remained.

Labor's influence, at least as measured by the unionization rate, peaked in 1989 at 23.3 percent. In 1986 it stood at 15.5 percent. By 1994 it was down to 16.3 percent. Despite all that Korea's trade union movement had achieved, it lost ground in the 1990s.

Looking directly at labor relations, we find evidence that suggests movement toward a new social compact. But there is also evidence that historical forms of labor repression remain, and government and business attitudes toward labor are little changed.

Korea is known worldwide as a global exporter of electronics, automobiles, ships, and wearing apparel. But in some settings Korea is also known as an exporter of poor labor relations. From export processing zones in the Dominican Republic to Korean foreign direct investments in Vietnam, there have been reports of labor abuse in Korean-owned factories. In Zhuhai, China, a 1996 *Asian Wall Street Journal* news story reported that a Korean factory boss ordered nearly 100 employees to kneel down before her as punishment after several assembly-line workers fell asleep during one of their breaks. The same story reported failure to pay back wages and general intimidation of the Chinese workers by Korean managers. The Zhuhai story is not an isolated case. Vietnamese labor officials reported that Korean firms accounted for half of all strikes and labor disputes among foreign firms in Vietnam during the 1990s. Yet Korea accounted for far less than half of all foreign direct investment.[1]

These same accounts by journalists and foreign labor ministries are quick to point out, however, that not all Korean firms behave in this manner. Poor labor relations are more common among smaller firms. Foreign direct investment by *chaebol* is more likely to conform with local practices and standards. Recognizing the existence of the problem, the Council of Korean Economic Organizations, representing five Korean business groups, issued a code of conduct for overseas investment that includes a call for respectful treatment of host country workers and cooperative labor management relations.

At home there is also mixed evidence of any fundamental departure from the repressive character of Korean labor relations. A noted authority on industrial relations in Korea concludes:

> Management response to the new industrial relations framework cannot be characterized by a single pattern. An aggressive anti-union stand [combined] with a union-free management strategy is seen in some sectors, while in other sectors, considerable efforts are made to cope with the new situation and to build a genuine partnership with the trade unions.[2]

One point of contention is the labor law, which was formulated prior to the late 1980s and in many ways remains essentially intact. Organized labor would like to see repeal of a number of provisions, including restrictions that enterprises be represented by only one union, that severely curtail involvement of third parties in collective bargaining, and that limit the political activity of trade unions. The Federation of Korean Employers has steadfastly opposed many of these changes. And the government, despite seeking and gaining admission to the International Labor Organization (ILO)—with the ILO advocating reform of Korea's labor law—has been slow to amend existing legislation.

Restriction of third-party participation in collective bargaining is an especially contentious issue and may result in a new wave of labor unrest. The Korea Confederation of Trade Unions (KCTU), heir to the radical union federations of the 1980s, boasts a membership of over 1.5 million and large influence among some of Korea's largest enterprise unions. But according to existing law, KCTU has no official recognition and, there-fore, unlike the Korean Federation of Trade Unions (FKTU), cannot participate in enterprise-level bargaining. Some in the government label KCTU subversive. Whether KCTU and its members will work for changes in bargaining practices through traditional political means or via a renewal of militant actions is unclear.[3]

Almost ten years have passed since the start of massive labor unrest in Korea. This period was brief, but its impact has been deep. Korean workers remain partners in their nation's economic growth. Real wages have risen quickly, and the workweek has been shortened. Union membership has grown absolutely and trade unions provide workers with a voice they formerly lacked. But attitudes among workers, managers, and government officials about the proper conduct of labor relations have been slower to change. The legal framework and institutions that are required of a modern industrial economy still must be developed. The 1990s have been less of a step backward than a pause in the evolution of an industrial relations system that will permit Korean society to prosper in the decades ahead.

NOTES

1. Chua Reginald, Jonathan Friedland, and In-Kyung Kim, "Some South Korean Plants Earn Ugly Reputation," *Asian Wall Street Journal Weekly*, July 22, 1996.

2. Fun-Koo Park, "Industrial Relations in Transition: Recent Develop-ments and Prospects," in L. Krause and Fun-Koo Park, *Social Issues in*

Korea: Korean and American Perspectives (Seoul: Korea Development Institute, 1993), p. 45.

3. Hoon, Shim-Jae, "Rocking the Boat: Militant Union Shakes Up Korea, Inc.," *Far Eastern Economic Review*, March 14, 1996.

Select Bibliography

Principal Statistical Sources

Bank of Korea. *Basic Wage Survey*. Seoul: Bank of Korea, 1967.

———. *Yearbook of Economic Statistics*. Seoul: Bank of Korea, 1988.

City of Taegu. *Taegu Statistical Yearbook*. 1988.

Economic Planning Board. *Korea Statistical Yearbook*. Seoul: Economic Planning Board.

———. *Population and Housing Census*. Seoul: Economic Planning Board.

———. *Urban Family Income and Expenditure Survey*. Seoul: Economic Planning Board.

———. *Survey (Census) of Mining and Manufacturing*. Seoul: Economic Planning Board.

———. *Annual Report on Economically Active Population*. Seoul: Economic Planning Board.

———. *Social Indicators in Korea*. 1988–1989.

International Labour Organization. *Yearbook of Labor Statistics*. Geneva: International Labour Organization, 1987.

Korea Reconstruction Bank. *Census of Mining and Manufacturing*. Seoul: Korea Reconstruction Bank, 1958.

Minimum Wage Council. *Manufacturing Wage Census*. Seoul: Minimum Wage Council, 1987.

Ministry of Agriculture, Fishery and Forestry. *Major Statistics of A.F.F.* Seoul: Ministry of Agriculture, Fishery and Forestry.

———. *Major Statistics of Agriculture*. Seoul: Ministry of Agriculture, Fishery and Forestry.

———. *Statistical Yearbook of A.F.F.* Seoul: Ministry of Agriculture, Fishery and Forestry.

Ministry of Commerce and Trade. *Industrial Estates*. Seoul: Ministry of Commerce and Trade.

Ministry of Construction. *Construction Handbook*. Seoul: Ministry of Construction.

Ministry of Health and Social Affairs. *Health and Social Statistics Yearbook*. Seoul: Ministry of Health and Social Affairs.

Ministry of Home Affairs. *Municipal Yearbook of Korea*. Seoul: Ministry of Home Affairs.

———. *Saemaul Undong*. 1987. Seoul: Ministry of Home Affairs. (In Korean).

Ministry of Labor. *Analysis of Occupational Injuries*. Seoul: Ministry of Labor, 1972–1989.

———. *Occupational Wage Survey*. Seoul: Ministry of Labor, 1971–1988.

———. *Yearbook of Labor Statistics*. Seoul: Ministry of Labor.

Ministry of Labor (Japan). *Basic Survey of Wage Structure*. Tokyo: Ministry of Labor.

U.S. Department of Labor, Bureau of International Labor Affairs. *Foreign Labor Trends: Korea*. Washington, D.C.: U.S. Government Printing Office, annual.

World Bank. *World Development Report, 1990*. Washington, D.C.: World Bank, 1990.

General Sources

Amsden, Alice. *Asia's Next Giant: South Korea and Late Industrialization*. New York: Oxford University Press, 1989.

———. "South Korea's Record Wage Rates: Labor in Late Industrialization." *Industrial Relations* 29, no. 1 (Winter 1990).

Asia Watch Committee. "Labor." In *Human Rights in Korea*. New York, Asia Watch Committee, January 1986.

Bai, Moo-Ki. *Education, Workers' Behavior and Earnings: A Case Study of Manufacturing Workers in Korea*. Seoul: Institute of Economic Research, Seoul National University, August 1977.

Ban, Sung-Hwan, Pal-Yong Moon, and Dwight H. Perkins. *Rural Development: Studies in the Modernization of the Republic of Korea, 1945–1975*. Cambridge: Council on East Asian Studies, Harvard University, 1980.

Bennett, John W., and Solomon B. Levine. "Industrialization and Social Deprivation: Welfare, Environment, and the Postindustrial Society in Japan." In Hugh Patrick, ed., *Japanese Industrialization and Its Social Consequences*. Berkeley: University of California Press, 1976.

Blinder, Alan S. "Wage Discrimination: Reduced Form and Structural Estimates." *Journal of Human Resources* (Fall 1973).

Bognanno, Mario. *Korea's Industrial Relations at the Turning Point.* KDI Working Paper 8816. Seoul: Korea Development Institute, December 1988.

Brandt, Vincent. "Korea." In George Lodge and Ezra Vogel, eds., *Ideology and National Competitiveness: An Analysis of Nine Countries.* Boston: Harvard Business School Press, 1987.

Castaneda, T., and F. K. Park. "Structural Adjustment and the Role of the Labor Market: The Case of Korea." In V. Corvo and S. M. Sah, eds., *Structural Adjustment in a Newly Industrialized Country: The Korean Experience.* Washington, D.C.: World Bank, 1992.

Chenery, H., and M. Syrquin. *Patterns of Development: 1950–1970.* New York, Oxford University Press for the World Bank, 1975.

Chira, S. "In Korean Factory, a Dream Is Reduced to Ashes." *New York Times,* April 6, 1988.

Choi, Jang-Jip. "A Corporatist Control of the Labor Union in South Korea." *Korean Social Science Journal* (1985).

————. *Labor and the Authoritarian State: Labor Unions in South Korean Manufacturing Industries, 1961–1980.* Seoul: Korea University Press, 1989.

Choi, Yang-Boo, and Dong-Pil Lee. "Policies for Developing Rural Income Sources: With an Emphasis on Rural Industrialization." Korea Rural Economy Institute, *The Direction for Development of Rural Income Sources.* 1984. (In Korean)

Choo, Hak-Chung. *Estimation of Size Distribution of Income and Its Sources of Change in Korea, 1982.* KDI Working Paper 8515. Seoul: Korea Development Institute, 1985.

————. *Widening Urban-Rural Income Differentials in Korea: A Re-examination.* KDI Working Paper 8205. Seoul: Korea Development Institute, August 1982.

————. and J. Yoon. "Size Distribution of Income in Korea, 1982: Its Estimation and Sources of Changes." *Korea Development Review* (1984). (In Korean)

Chung, Young-Il. "An Analysis of Migration by the Census Data." In I. H. Choi, Y. I. Chung, and Y. C. Byun, eds., *Migration and Socioeconomic Developments.* Seoul: KIPH and EPB, 1986. (In Korean)

Clifford, M. "Labour Strikes Out." *Far Eastern Economic Review,* August 27, 1987.

Davies, James C. "Toward a Theory of Revolution." *American Sociological Review* 27 (February 1962).

Dervis, K., and P. Petri. "The Macroeconomics of Successful Development: What Are the Lessons?" In S. Fischer, ed., *NBER Macroeconomics Annual 1987*. Cambridge: MIT Press, 1987.

Deyo, Frederic. *Beneath the Miracle: Labor Subordination in the New Asian Industrialism*. Berkeley: University of California Press, 1989.

————. Stephan Haggard, and Koo Hagen. "Labor in the Political Economy of East Asian Industrialization." *Bulletin of Concerned Asian Scholars* 19, no. 2 (1987).

Dornbusch, R., and Y. C. Park. *Korean Growth Policy*. Brookings Papers on Economic Activity 2. Washington, D.C.: Brookings, 1987.

Fields, Gary S. "Industrialization and Employment in Hong Kong, Korea, Singapore, and Taiwan." In Walter Galenson, ed., *Foreign Trade and Investment: Economic Growth in the Newly Industrializing Asian Countries*. Madison: University of Wisconsin Press, 1985.

Freeman, Richard B. *The Changing Economic Value of Higher Education in Developed Countries: A Report to the OECD*. Discussion Paper 874. Cambridge: Harvard Institute of Economic Research, January 1982.

————. and James Medoff. *What Do Unions Do?* New York: Basic Books, 1984.

Galenson, Walter. "The Japanese Labor Market." In H. Patrick and H. Rosovsky, eds., *Asia's New Giant: How the Japanese Economy Works*. Washington, D.C.: Brookings Institution, 1976.

Han, Sung-Joo, and Yung Chul Park. "South Korea: Democratization at Last." In James Morley, ed., *Driven by Growth: Political Change in the Asia-Pacific Region*. Armonk, N.Y.: M. E. Sharpe, 1993.

Hashimoto, M., and J. Raisan. "Employment, Tenure, and Earnings Profiles in Japan." *American Economic Review* 75 (1985).

Hazama, Hiroshi. "Historical Changes in the Life Style of Industrial Workers." In Hugh Patrick, ed., *Japanese Industrialization and Its Social Consequences*. Berkeley: University of California Press, 1976.

Henle, Peter, and Paul Ryscavage. "The Distribution of Earned Income Among Men and Women, 1958–77." *Monthly Labor Review* (April 1980).

Hirschmann, A. O. "The Changing Tolerance for Income Inequality in the Course of Economic Development." *Quarterly Journal of Economics* 87 (November 1973).

————. *Exit, Voice, and Loyalty*. Cambridge: Harvard University Press, 1971.

Hong, Doo-Seung. "A Preliminary Analysis of Korean Social Stratification." *Tradition and Change in Korean Society*. Seoul: Bum-Mun Sa, 1983.

————. *A Study of Social Stratification by the Analysis of Occupational Structure*. Social Sciences and Policy Studies 5, no. 3. Seoul National University, 1983.

Hong, Seung-Chick. *A Study on Intellectuals' Value-Orientations*. Seoul: Sam-Young Co., 1972.

Hong, Sung-Woong. "Balancing Equity and Efficiency in Regional Policy." In Myong-Chan Hwang and Harry W. Richardson, eds., *Urban and Regional Policy in Korea and International Experiences*. Seoul: Kon-Kuk University Press, 1987.

Hong, Won-Tak. "Korean Economy at Crossroad." *Sasang Quarterly* 1 (Summer 1989).

Hunnicutt, Benjamin. *Work Without End: Abandoning Shorter Hours for the Right to Work*. Philadelphia: Temple University Press, 1988.

Hwang Myong-Chan, and Jin-Ho Choi. "Evolution of the Settlement System in Korea: A Historical Perspective." In Myong-Chan Hwang and Harry W. Richardson, eds., *Urban and Regional Policy in Korea and International Experiences*. Seoul: Kon-Kuk University Press, 1987.

Jho, Jung-Jay. "An Assessment of Korean Rural Industrialization Policies." *Korea Spatial Planning Review* 10 (September 1988). (In Korean)

Jones, F. L. "On Decomposing the Wage Gap: A Critical Comment on Blinder's Method." *Journal of Human Resources* (Winter 1983).

Kakwani, Nanak. *Income Inequality and Poverty: Methods of Estimation and Policy Applications*. Oxford: Oxford University Press, 1980.

Kim, Dae-Il, and R. Topel. "Labor Markets and Economic Growth: Lessons from Korea's Industrialization." In R. Freeman and L. Katz, eds., *Differences and Changes in Wage Structure*. Chicago: University of Chicago Press, 1995.

Kim, Dae-Jung. "Korea's Labor Relations Policy." *Korean-American Relations Review*. Monmouth Junction, New Jersey: Alliance for Democracy in Korea, Vol. II, No. 2, 1984.

Kim, Jong-Gie. "The Effect of Infrastructure Investment on Regional Development in Korea, 1970–1985." Korea Development Review 9, no. 3 (Fall 1987). (In Korean)

————. *Rural Industrialization in Korea: Current Status and Future Policy Directions*. KDI Working Paper. Seoul: Korea Development Institute, September 1983.

————. and Il-Chung Hwang. *Characteristics of Rural Industries and Policies for Rural Industrialization*. Seoul: Korea Development Institute, 1987. (In Korean)

————. Kwan-Young Kim, and Jae-Young Son. *Problems of Urbanization and the Growth of Seoul, Korea.* Seoul: Korea Development Institute, 1991.

Kim, Kwang-Suk, and Michael Roemer. *Growth and Structural Transformation: Studies in the Modernization of the Republic of Korea, 1945–1975.* Cambridge: Council on East Asian Studies, Harvard University, 1979.

Kim, Kyoung-Dong. "Occupational Values and Social Structure." *Social Sciences and Policy Studies* 5, no. 3 (1983).

Kim, Min-Ha. "Political Attitudes of Koreans." *Chung-Ang Journal of Social Sciences* 1 (1987).

Kim, Soo-Kon. "Is the Japanese System of Lifetime Employment Applicable to a Developing Country Such As Korea?" Paper presented at the Sixth World Congress of International Industrial Relations Association, Kyoto, Japan, March 29–31, 1983.

Kim, Sung-Kuk. "Industrialization and Industrial Conflicts." In Korean Sociological Association, ed., *A Study of Conflicts in Korea.* Seoul: Korean Sociological Association, 1985.

Kim, Young-Hwa. "Education and Male-Female Earnings Inequality in the Structured Labor Markets: A Case Study of Korea." Ph.D. dissertation, Stanford University, 1986.

Kim, Young-Mo. *A Study of Social Stratification in Korea.* Seoul: Il-Chokak, 1982.

————. "Social Class Structure and Its Change in Korea." *Korean Journal of Sociology* 19 (1985).

————. "Sense of Social Inequality Among Koreans." *Chung-Ang Journal of Social Sciences* 1 (1987).

Koo, Hagen. "A Preliminary Analysis of Social Class Structure of Contemporary Korean Society." *Reinterpretation of Korean Society* 1 (1985).

————. "The State, Industrial Structure, and Labor Politics: Comparison of South Korea and Taiwan." In Korean Sociological Association, ed., *Industrial East Asia,* 1989.

————. "Transformation of the Korean Class Structure: The Impact of Independent Development." In Robert Robinson, ed., *Research in Social Stratification and Mobility* 4. Greenwich, Conn.: JAI Press, 1985.

————. *Work and Class in the New East Asian Capitalism.* Forthcoming.

————. and Doo-Seung Hong. "Class and Income Inequality in Korea." *American Sociological Review* 45 (1980).

Korean Social Missionary Council. *The Living Conditions of Laborers: A Survey of Laborers' Wages and Living*. Seoul: Poolbit Publishers, 1985.

Koshiro, Kazutoshi. "The Quality of Working Life in Japanese Factories." In Taishiro Shirai, ed., *Contemporary Industrial Relations in Japan*. Madison: University of Wisconsin Press, 1983.

Kotaro, Tsujimura. "The Effect of Reductions in Working Hours on Productivity." In Shunsaku Nishikawa, ed., *The Labor Market in Japan*. Tokyo: University of Tokyo Press, 1980.

Kravis, I., A. Heston, and R. Summers. "New Insights into the Structure of the World Economy." *Review of Income and Wealth* 30 (December 1981).

Kuznets, Paul. "An East Asian Model of Economic Development: Japan, Taiwan, and South Korea." *Economic Development and Cultural Change* 36, no. 3 (Supplement) (April 1988).

Kuznets, S. *Modern Economic Growth: Rate, Structure, and Spread*. New Haven: Yale University Press, 1966.

Kwon, Won-Yong. "Regional Development Policies and Strategies for the Sixth Economic and Social Development Plan (1987–1991)." In Myong-Chan Hwang and Harry W. Richardson, eds., *Urban and Regional Policy in Korea and International Experiences*. Seoul: Kon-Kuk University Press, 1987.

Launius, Michael. "The State and Industrial Labor in South Korea." *Bulletin of Concerned Asian Scholars* 16, no. 4 (1984).

Lee, Dae-Keun. "Economic Growth and Structural Disequilibrium." In Korean Social Science Research Council, ed., *Social Change and Problems*. Seoul: Bub-Mun Sa, 1986.

Lee, Han-Soon, and Lee Woo-Rhee. "A Qualitative Study on Changing Patterns of Internal Migration in Korea, 1960–1980." *Journal of Population Studies* 24 (1983).

Lee, Hyo-Sun. "Attitudes Toward Labor Disputes." *Chung-Ang Journal of Social Sciences* 1 (1987).

Lee, Jeong-Sik. "Regional Development Policies in Korea, Retrospect and Prospects." *Korea Spatial Planning Review* 10 (September 1988).

Lee, Kak-Bum. "Industrial Development and Industrial Conflicts." In Korean Sociological Association, ed., *Where Korean Society Is Headed*. Seoul: Korean Sociological Association, 1983.

Lee, Kyu-Eok. "Causes of and Policies on the Concentration of Economic Power." Shinpyung Forum. May 1989.

Lee, Young-Hee. "White Collar Workers at Big Business." In Korea Social Research Institute, *A Study on Korean Workers*, vol. 1. Seoul: Baiksan Publisher, 1989. (In Korean)

Leipziger, Danny, et al. *The Distribution of Income and Wealth in Korea.* EDI Development Studies. Washington, D.C.: World Bank, 1992.

Lewis, Arthur. *The Theory of Economic Growth.* London: George Allen & Unwin, 1955.

Lim, Hy-Sop. *Social Equality and Development.* Seoul: Chung-Um Sa, 1986.

Lim, Young-Il, et al. "The Consciousness of Production Workers at Big Business." In Korea Social Research Institute, *A Study on Korean Workers*, vol. 1. Seoul: Baiksan Publisher, 1989. (In Korean)

Lindauer, David L. *Labor Market Behavior in the Republic of Korea: An Analysis of Wages and Their Impact on the Economy.* World Bank Staff Working Papers No. 641. Washington, D.C.: World Bank, 1984.

Malpezzi, S., and S. Mayo. "The Demand for Housing in Developing Countries: Empirical Estimates from Household Data." *Economic Development and Cultural Change* 35, no. 4 (July 1987).

Mason, Edward S., et al. *The Economic and Social Modernization of the Republic of Korea: Studies in the Modernization of the Republic of Korea, 1945–1975.* Cambridge: Council on East Asian Studies, Harvard University, 1980.

McGinn, Noel, et al. *Education and Development in Korea: Studies in the Modernization of the Republic of Korea: 1945–1975.* Cambridge: Council on East Asian Studies, Harvard University, 1980.

Mills, Edwin S., and Byung-nak Song. *Urbanization and Urban Problems: Studies in the Modernization of the Republic of Korea, 1945–1975.* Cambridge: Council on East Asian Studies, Harvard University, 1980.

Mincer, Jacob, and Yoshio Higuchi. "Wage Structures and Labor Turnover in the United States and Japan." *Journal of the Japanese and International Economies* 2 (1988).

Moon, Pal-Yong, et al. *Rural Development in Korea.* Seoul: Korea Development Institute, 1981. (In Korean)

Owen, John D. *Reduced Working Hours: Cure for Unemployment or Economic Burden?* Baltimore: Johns Hopkins University Press, 1989.

———. *Working Hours.* Lexington, Mass.: D. C. Heath and Company, 1979.

Park, Fun-Koo, and Se-Il Park. *Wage Structure in Korea.* Seoul: Korea Development Institute, 1984.

Park, Se-Il. *Compensation in the Public Enterprises in Korea*. Policy Research Paper 86-10. Seoul: Korea Development Institute, 1986. (In Korean)

————. "Labor Issues in Korea's Future." *World Development* 16, no. 1 (1988).

————. "Labor Policy in Korea: Its Features and Problems." Paper presented at the Conference on the Role of the State in Economic Development, UCLA, August 1987.

————. "Public Sector Compensation in Korea." *Korea Development Review* 6, no. 2 (March 1984). (In Korean)

Park, Young-Ki. "Economic Democratization and Industrial Relations in Korea with Special Reference to the Role of Unions." Paper presented at International Symposium on Economic Democracy and Industrial Relations, Seoul, Korea, June 16–17, 1988.

————. *Labor and Industrial Relations in Korea: System and Practice*. Institute for Labor and Management Studies 6. Seoul: Sogang University Press, 1979.

Peattie, L. "An Idea in Good Currency and How It Grew: The Informal Sector." *World Development* 15, no. 7 (July 1987).

Rodgers, Ronald. "An Exclusionary Labor Regime Under Pressure: The Changes in Labor Relations in the Republic of Korea since Mid-1987." *UCLA Pacific Basin Law Journal* 8, no. 1 (Spring 1990).

Shirai, Taishiro. *Contemporary Industrial Relations in Japan*. Madison: University of Wisconsin Press, 1983.

Sim, Young-Hee. *A Study on Relative Deprivation and Social Classes*. Report submitted to the Korea Ministry of Education, 1987.

Song, Byung-Nak. *The Rise of the Korean Economy*. Hong Kong: Oxford University Press, 1990.

Song, Dae-Hee, and Byong-Suh Yoo. *Structural Adjustment of Agriculture in the Age of Industrialization*. Seoul: Korea Development Institute, 1985. (In Korean)

Song, Ho-Keun. "State and the Working-Class Labor Market in South Korea, 1961–1987." Ph.D. dissertation, Harvard University, 1989.

Suh, Joong-Suk. "The Deadend of Human Rights: The Scenes of Industrial Accidents." *Shin-Dong-Ah* (July 1987).

Suh, Kwan-Mo. *Class Composition and Class Differentiation in Contemporary Korean Society*. Seoul: Han-Ul, 1984.

Suh, Sang-Mok, et al. *Current State of Poverty and Policies on the Poor*. Seoul: Korea Development Research Institute, 1981.

Summers, R., and A. Heston. "Improved International Comparisons of Real Product and Its Composition: 1950–1980." *Review of Income and Wealth* 30, no. 2 (June 1984).

Syrquin, M., and H. Chenery. *Patterns of Development, 1950 to 1983*. World Bank Discussion Paper 41. Washington, D.C.: World Bank, 1989.

West, J. "Review Essay: The Suboptimal 'Miracle' of South Korean State Capitalism." *Bulletin of Concerned Asian Scholars* 19, no. 3 (1987).

Wilkinson, Barry. *Labour and Industry in the Asia Pacific*. Berlin: Walter de Gruyter, 1994.

World Bank. *Korea: Spatial Strategy Review*. Washington, D.C.: World Bank, 1986.

———. *1995 World Development Report: Workers in an Integrating World*. Washington, D.C.: World Bank, 1995.

Yamamoto, Kiyoshi. *Wages and Working Hours in Japan*. Tokyo: Tokyo University Press, 1982. (In Japanese)

Yoo, Hee-Joung. "A Study on the Social Consciousness of the Middle Class." *Korean Journal of Sociology* 22 (1988).

Index

DATE DUE

~~DEC 0 1 1997~~		
~~JAN 1 2 1998~~		
~~FEB 2 0 1998~~		
~~APR 0 3 1998~~		
~~MAY 1 5 1998~~		
~~JUN 1998~~		
		Printed in USA

HIGHSMITH #45230